The Father and Daughter, a Tale. With an Epistle from the Maid of Corinth to Her Lover; and Other Poetical Pieces
by Amelia Opie

Address:
HardPress
8345 NW 66TH ST #2561
MIAMI FL 33166-2626
USA
Email: info@hardpress.net

THE

THE

FATHER AND DAUGHTER,

A TALE, IN PROSE.

—" Thy fweet reviving fmiles might cheer defpair,
On the pale lips detain the parting breath,
And bid hope bloffom in the fhades of death."

Mrs. BARBAULD.

THE

FATHER AND DAUGHTER,

A TALE, IN PROSE:

WITH

AN EPISTLE

FROM

THE MAID OF CORINTH TO HER LOVER;

AND

OTHER POETICAL PIECES.

By Mrs. OPIE.

LONDON:

Printed by Davis, Wilks, and Taylor, Chancery-Lane;
AND SOLD BY LONGMAN AND REES, PATERNOSTER-ROW.

1801.

DEDICATION.

_____

TO

DR. ALDERSON, OF NORWICH.

_____

DEAR SIR,

  IN dedicating this Publication to you, I follow in fome meafure the example of thofe nations who devoted to their gods the firſt fruits of the genial feafons which they derived from their bounty.

To you I owe whatever of cultivation my mind has received; and the firſt fruits of that mind to you I dedicate.

Befides, having endeavoured in " THE FATHER AND DAUGHTER" to exhibit a

A 2   picture

picture of the moſt perfect parental affection, to whom could I dedicate it with ſo
much propriety as to you, ſince, in de-
ſcribing a good father, I had only to de-
lineate my own ?

Allow me to add, full of gratitude for
years of tenderneſs and indulgence on your
part, but feebly repaid even by every poſſible
ſentiment of filial regard on mine, that the
ſatisfaction I ſhall experience if my Publication be favourably received by the world,
will not proceed from the mere gratification of my ſelf-love, but from the conviction I ſhall feel that my ſucceſs as an
Author is productive of pleaſure to you.

AMELIA OPIE.

BERNERS STREET,
1800.

TO THE READER.

———

IT is not without confiderable apprehenfion that I offer myfelf as an avowed Author at the bar of public opinion,....and that apprehenfion is heightened by its being the general cuftom to give indifcriminately the name of NOVEL to every thing in Profe that comes in the fhape of a Story, however fimple it be in its conftruction, and humble in its pretenfions.

By this means, the following Publication is in danger of being tried by a ftandard according to which it was never intended to be made, and to be criticifed for wanting thofe merits which it was never meant to poffefs.

I there-

I therefore beg leave to say, in justice to myself, that I know "THE FATHER AND DAUGHTER" is wholly devoid of those attempts at strong character, comic situation, bustle, and variety of incident, which constitute a NOVEL, and that its highest pretensions are, to be a SIMPLE, MORAL TALE.

ERRATA.

P. 17, l. 8, for " that" read " this information". P. 35, l. 17, for " support" read " bear". P. 38, l. 13, for " replied he" read " replied the other". P. 42, l. 18, for " or" read " and". P. 44, l. 20, for " part as good friends as ever" read " part good friends". P. 47, l. 24, for " or the outside" read " or on the outside". P. 51, l. 6, for " trackless" read " lonely". P. 63, l. 5, for " tearful" read " tearless". P. 74, l. 20, for " again" read " you shall". P. 99, l. 13, for " Agnes" read " she". P. 108, l. 4, for " so she did" read " so did she". P. 110, l. 14, for " recollection" read " idea". P. 157, l. 6, for " he suffered" read " of his suffering". P. 181, l. 9, for " her father" read " Fitzhenry". P. 198, l. 13, for " child" read " Edward". P. 198, l. 30, for " of a villain" read " of villain".

FATHER AND DAUGHTER.

A TALE.

THE night was dark—the wind blew keenly over the frozen and rugged heath, when Agnes, preffing her moaning child to her bofom, was travelling on foot to her father's habitation.

" Would to God I had never left it !" fhe exclaimed, as home and all its enjoyments rofe in fancy to her view :—and I think my readers will be ready to join in the exclamation, when they hear the poor wanderer's hiftory.

Agnes Fitzhenry was the only child, of a refpectable merchant in a country town,

B   who,

who, háving loft his wife when his daughter was very young, refolved for her fake to form no fecond connection. To the fteady, manly affection of a father, Fitzhenry joined the fond anxieties and endearing attentions of a mother; and his parental care was amply repaid by the love and amiable qualities of Agnes. He was not rich, yet the profits of his trade were fuch as to enable him to beftow every poffible expenfe on his daughter's education, and to lay up a confiderable fum yearly for her future fupport : whatever elfe he could fpare from his own abfolute wants, he expended in procuring comforts and pleafures for her.—" What an excellent father that man is!" was the frequent exclamation among his acquaintance—" and what an excellent child he has! well may he be proud of her," was as commonly the anfwer to it. Nor was this to be wondered at :—Agnes united to extreme beauty of face and perfon every accomplifhment that belongs to her own fex, and a great degree of that ftrength of

mind

mind. and capacity for acquiring Knowledge fuppofed to belong exclufively to
the other.

For this combination of rare qualities
Agnes was admired;—for her fweetnefs of
temper, her willingnefs to oblige, her feeming unconfciousnefs of her own merits, and
her readinefs to commend the merits of
others,—for thefe ftill rarer qualities, Agnes
was beloved: and fhe feldom formed an
acquaintance without at the fame time fecuring a friend.

But fhort was thy triumph, fweet Agnes,
and long was thy affliction!

Her father thought he loved her (and
perhaps he was right) as never father loved
a child before; and Agnes thought fhe
loved him as child never before loved father
—"I will not marry, but live fingle for my
father's fake," fhe often faid;—but fhe altered her determination when her heart,
hitherto unmoved by the addreffes of the
other fex, was affailed by an officer in the

B 2   Guards

Guards who came to recruit in the town
in which she refided.

Clifford, as I fhall call him, had not
only a fine figure and a graceful addrefs,
but talents rare and various, and powers
of converfation fo fafcinating, that the
woman he had betrayed forgot her wrongs
in his prefence; and the creditor, who
came to dun him for the payment of
debts already incurred, went away eager
to oblige him by letting him incur ftill
more. — Fatal perverfion of uncommon
abilities! This man, who might have
taught a nation to look up to him as
its beft pride and profperity, and its beft
hope in adverfity, made no other ufe of
his talents than to betray the unwary of
both fexes, the one to fhame, the other
to pecuniary difficulties; and he whofe
mind was capacious enough to have imagined fchemes to aggrandize his native
country, the flave of fordid felfifhnefs,
never looked beyond his own temporary

and

and petty benefit, and sat down contented with the achievements of the day, if he had overreached a credulous tradesman, or beguiled an unsuspecting woman.

But to accomplish even these paltry triumphs, great knowledge of the human heart was necessary—a power of discovering the prevailing foible in those on whom he had designs, and of converting their imagined security into their real danger. He soon discovered that Agnes, who was rather inclined to doubt her possessing in an uncommon degree the good qualities which she really had, valued herself, with not unusual blindness, on those which she had not. She thought herself endowed with great power to read the characters of those with whom she associated, when she had even not discrimination enough to understand her own : and, while she imagined it was not in the power of others to deceive her, she was constantly in the habit of deceiving herself.

Clifford was not slow to avail himself of

this

this weaknefs in his intended victim ; and, while he taught her to believe none of his faults had efcaped her obfervation, with hers he had made himfelf thoroughly acquainted.——But not content with making her faults fubfervient to his views, he preffed her virtues alfo into his fervice : and her affection for her father, that ftrong hold, fecure in which, Agnes would have defied the moft violent affaults of temptation, he contrived fhould be the means of her defeat.

I have been thus minute in detailing the various and feducing powers which Clifford poffeffed, not becaufe he will be a principal figure in my narrative, for, on the contrary, the chief characters in it are the father and daughter, but in order to excufe as much as poffible the ftrong attachment which he excited in Agnes.

" Love," fays Mrs. Inchbald, whofe accurate acquaintance with human nature can be equalled only by the humour with which fhe defcribes its follies, and the unrivalled

rivalled pathos with which fhe exhibits its diftreffes—" Love, however rated by many as the chief paffion of the heart, is but a poor dependant, a retainer on the other paffions—admiration, gratitude, refpect, efteem, pride in the object;—diveft the boafted fenfation of thefe, and it is no more than the impreffion of a twelvemonth, by courtefy, or vulgar error, called love.*"— And of all thefe ingredients was the paffion of Agnes compofed. For the graceful per-fon and manner of Clifford fhe felt admi-ration, and her gratitude was excited by her obferving that, while he was an object of attention to every one wherever he ap-peared, his attentions were exclufively di-rected to herfelf; and that he who, from his rank and accomplifhments, might have laid claim to the hearts even of the brighteft daughters of fafhion, in the gayeft fcenes of the metropolis, feemed to have no higher ambition than to appear amiable in the eyes

* Nature and Art, vol. i. p. 142.

of

of Agnes, the humble toaſt of an obſcure country town ; while his ſuperiority of under-ſtanding, and brilliancy of talents, called forth her reſpect, and his apparent virtues her eſteem ; and when to this high idea of the qualities of the man, was added a knowledge of his high birth and great expectations, it is no wonder that ſhe alſo felt the laſt men-tioned, and often perhaps the greateſt, ex-citement to love, " pride in the object."

When Clifford began to pay thoſe marked attentions to Agnes, which ought always on due encouragement from the woman to whom they are addreſſed to be followed by an offer of marriage, he contrived to make himſelf as much diſliked by the father, as admired by the daughter ; yet his manage-ment was ſo artful, that Fitzhenry could not give a ſufficient reaſon for his diſlike ; he could only declare its exiſtence ; and for the firſt time in her life, Agnes learned to think her father unjuſt, and capricious. Thus, while Clifford enſured an acceptance of his addreſſes from Agnes, he at the ſame

time

time fecured a rejection of them from Fitzhenry; and this was the object of his
wifhes, as he had a decided averfion to
marriage, and knew befides that marrying
Agnes would difappoint all his ambitious
profpects in life, and bring on him the
eternal difpleafure of his father.

At length, after playing for fome time
with her hopes and fears, Clifford requefted
Fitzhenry to fanction with his approbation
his addreffes to his daughter; and Fitzhenry, as he expected, coldly and firmly
declined the honour of his alliance. But
when Clifford mentioned, as if unguardedly, that he hoped to prevail on his father
to approve the marriage after it had taken
place, if not before, Fitzhenry proudly told
him he thought his daughter much too
good to be fmuggled into the family of any
one; while Clifford, piqued in his turn at
the warmth of Fitzhenry's expreffions, and
the dignity of his manner, left him, exulting fecretly in the confcioufnefs that he

had

had his revenge—for he knew the heart of Agnes was irrecoverably his.

Agnes heard from her lover that his suit was rejected, with agonies as violent as he appeared to feel.——"What!" exclaimed she, " can that affectionate father, who has till now anticipated my wishes, disappoint me in the wish dearest to my heart ?"   In the midst of her first agitation her father entered the room, and, with " a countenance more in sorrow than in anger," began to expostulate with her on the impropriety of the connection which she was desirous of forming.——He represented to her the very slender income Clifford possessed—the inconvenience to which an officer's wife is exposed, and the little chance there is for a man's making a constant and domestic husband who has been brought up in an idle profession, and accustomed to habits of intemperance, expense, and irregularity :——

" But above all," said he, " how is it possible

possible that you could ever condescend to accept the addresses of a man whose father, he himself owns, will never sanction them with his approbation?"——Alas! Agnes could plead no excuse but that she was in love, and she had too much sense to urge such a plea to her father—" Believe me," he continued, " I speak thus from the most disinterested consideration of your interest ; for, painful as the idea of parting with you must be to me, I am certain I should not shrink from the bitter trial, whenever my misery would be your happiness (here his voice faltered) ; but in this case I am certain, that by refusing my consent to your wishes I ensure your future comfort ; and in a cooler moment you will be of the same opinion." Agnes shook her head, and turned away in tears. " Nay, hear me, my child," resumed Fitzhenry, " you know I am no tyrant; and if, after time and absence have been tried in order to conquer your unhappy passion, it remain unchanged, then, in defiance of my judgment, I will

consent

confent to your marriage with Mr. Clifford, provided his father confent likewife ; for, unlefs he does, I never will :—and if you have not pride and refolution enough to be the guardian of your own dignity, I muft guard it for you ; but I am fure there will be no need of my interference ; and Agnes Fitzhenry would fcorn to be clandeftinely the wife of any man."

Agnes thought fo too—and Fitzhenry fpoke this in fo mild and affectionate a manner, and in a tone fo expreffive of fup-preffed wretchednefs, which the bare idea of parting with her had occafioned him, that, for the moment, fhe forgot every thing but her father, and the vaft debt of love and gratitude fhe owed him, and throwing herfelf into his arms fhe protefted her entire, nay cheerful, acquiefcence in his determination.—" Promife me, then," replied Fitzhenry, " that you will never fee Mr. Clifford more, if you can avoid it—he has the tongue of Belial, and if———" Here Agnes indignantly interrupted him with reproaches

reproaches for fuppofing her fo weak as to be in danger of being feduced into a violation of her duty ; and fo ftrong were the terms in which fhe expreffed herfelf, that her father entreated her pardon for having thought fuch a promife neceffary.

The next day Clifford did not venture to call at the houfe, but he watched the door till he faw Agnes come out alone, and then having joined her, he obtained from her a full account of the converfation fhe had had with Fitzhenry ; when, to her great furprife, he drew conclufions from it, which fhe had never imagined poffible. He faw, or pretended to fee, in Fitzhenry's rejection of his offers, not merely a diflike of her marrying him, but a defign to prevent her marrying at all ; and as a defign like this was felfifh in the laft degree, and ought not to be complied with, he thought it would be kinder in her to difobey her father, and marry the man of her heart, than, by indulging him once, flatter him with the hope fhe would do it again,

again, till by this means, the day of her marrying, when it came at laft, would burft on him with tenfold horrors.——The refult of this fpecious reafoning, enforced by tears, careffes, and proteftations, was, that fhe had better go off to Scotland immediately with him, and truft to time, neceffity, and their parents' affection, to fecure their forgivenefs.

Agnes the firft time heard thefe arguments, and this propofal, with the difdain they merited ; but, alas ! fhe did not refolve to avoid all opportunity of hearing them a fecond time : but, vain of the refolution fhe had fhown on this firft trial, fhe was not averfe to ftand another, delighted to find that fhe had not overrated her ftrength, when fhe reproached Fitzhenry for his want of confidence in it. The confequence is obvious :——again and again fhe heard Clifford argue in favour of an elopement ; and, though fhe ftill retained virtue fufficient to withhold her confent, fhe every day faw frefh reafon to believe he argued on good grounds,

grounds, and to think that parent whofe whole ftudy had been, till now, her gratification, was, in this inftance at leaft, the flave of unwarrantable felfifhnefs.———

At laft, finding neither time, reflection, nor even a temporary abfence, had the flighteft effect on her attachment, but that it gained new force every day, fhe owned that nothing but the dread of making her father unhappy, withheld her from liftening to Clifford's propofal :—'twas true, fhe faid, pride forbade it, but the woman who could liften to the dictates of pride, knew nothing of love but the name.——This was the moment for Clifford to urge more ftrongly than ever that the elopement was the moft effectual means of fecuring her father's happinefs, as well as her own ; till at laft her judgment became the dupe of her wifhes ; and, fancying fhe was following the dictates of filial affection, when fhe was in reality the helplefs victim of paffion, fhe yielded to the perfuafions of a villain, and fet off with him to Scotland.

When

When Fitzhenry firſt heard of her flight, he ſat for hours abſorbed in a ſort of dumb anguiſh, far more eloquent than words. At length he burſt into exclamations againſt her ingratitude for all the love and care he had beſtowed on her; and the next moment he exclaimed, with tears of tenderneſs, " Poor girl ! ſhe is not uſed to commit faults ; how miſerable ſhe will be when ſhe comes to reflect ! and how ſhe will long for my forgiveneſs ! and, O yes ! I am ſure I ſhall long as ardently to forgive her !"— Then his arms were folded in fancy round his child, whom he pictured to himſelf confeſſing her marriage to him, and upon her knees imploring his pardon.—But day after day came, and no letter from the fugitives, acknowledging their error, and begging his bleſſing on their union—for no union had taken place. When Clifford and Agnes had been conveyed as faſt as four horſes could carry them one hundred miles towards Gretna-green, and had ordered freſh horſes, Clifford ſtarted, as he looked

looked at his pocket-book, and, with well-diffembled confternation, exclaimed " What can we do ? I have brought the wrong pocket-book, and have not money enough to carry us above a hundred and odd miles further on the North road !"— Agnes was overwhelmed with grief and apprehenfion at that information, but did not for an inftant fufpect the fact was other-wife than as Clifford ftated it to be.

As I before obferved, Agnes piqued her-felf on her knowledge of characters, and fhe judged of them frequently by the rules of phyfiognomy—fhe had ftudied voices too, as well as countenances ;—was it poffible, then, that Agnes, who had from Clifford's voice and countenance pronounced him all that was ingenuous, honourable, and manly, could fufpect him capable of artifice ? could fhe, retracting her pretenfions to penetra-tion, believe fhe had put herfelf in the power of a defigning libertine ? No—vanity and felf-love forbade this falutary fufpicion to enter her imagination ; and, without one fcruple,

fcruple, or one reproach, fhe acceded to the plan Clifford propofed, as the only one likely to obviate their difficulties, and procure them moft fpeedily an opportunity of folemnizing their marriage.

Deluded Agnes ! you might have known that the honourable lover is as fearful to commit the honour of his miftrefs even in appearance, as fhe herfelf can be ; that his care and anxiety to fcreen her even from the breath of fufpicion are ever on the watch ; and that therefore, had Clifford's defigns been fuch as virtue would approve, he would have put it out of the power of accident to prevent your immediate marriage, and expofe your fair fame to the whifper of calumny.

To London they fet forward, and were driven to a hotel in the Adelphi, whence Clifford went out in fearch of lodgings ; and, having met with convenient apartments at the weft end of the town, he conducted to them the penfive, and already repentant Agnes.—" Under what name and title," faid Agnes, " am I to be introduced to the woman of the houfe ?"—" As my intended wife," cried her lover, preffing her to his bofom, "and in a few days— though to me they will appear ages—you will give me a right to call you by that tender name."—" In a few days !" exclaimed Agnes, withdrawing from his embrace, " cannot the marriage take place tomorrow ?"—" Impoffible !" replied Clifford, " you are not of age—I can't procure a licenfe—but I have taken thefe lodgings for a month—we will have the banns publifhed, and be married at the parifh church."

To this arrangement, againft which her delicacy and every feeling revolted, Agnes would fain have objected in the ftrongeft manner; but, unable to urge any reafons for her objection, except fuch as feemed to imply diftruft of her own virtue, fhe fubmitted, in mournful filence, to the plan ; and, with a heart then for the firft time tortured with a fenfe of degradation, fhe took
poffeffion

poffeffion of her apartment, and Clifford returned to his hotel, meditating with fa- vage delight on the fuccefs of his plans, and on the triumph which, he fancied, awaited him.

Agnes paffed the night in fleeplefs agi- tation, now forming and now rejecting fchemes to obviate the danger which muft accrue to her character, if not to her ho- nour, by remaining for a whole month ex- pofed to the feductions of a man, whom fhe had but too fatally convinced of his power over her heart; and the refult of her reflections was, that fhe fhould infift on his leaving town, and not returning till he came to lead her to the altar. Happy would it have been for Agnes, had fhe ad- hered to this refolution, but vanity and felf-confidence again interfered :—" What have I to fear?" faid Agnes to herfelf—"am I fo fallen in my own efteem that I dare not expofe myfelf even to a fhadow of temptation ?—No—I will not think fo meanly of my virtue;—the woman that is afraid

afraid of being difhonoured is half overcome already ; and I will meet with boldnefs the trials I cannot avoid."

O vanity ! thou haft much to anfwer
for !—I am convinced that, were we to
trace up to their fource all the moft painful and degrading events of our lives, wo
fhould find moft of them to have their
origin in the gratified fuggeftions of vanity.

It is not my intention to follow Agnes
through the fucceffion of mortifications,
embarraffments, temptations, and ftruggles,
which preceded her undoing (for, fecure
as fhe thought herfelf in her own ftrength,
and the honour of her lover, fhe became at
laft a prey to her feducer) ; it is fufficient
that I explain the circumftances which led
to her being in a cold winter's night houfe-
lefs, and unprotected, a melancholy wanderer towards the houfe of her father.

Before the expiration of the month, Clifford had triumphed over the virtue of Agnes,
and foon after he received orders to join his
regiment, as it was going to be fent on im-

4   mediate

mediate fervice.—" But you will return to me before you embark, in order to make me your wife ?" faid the half diftracted Agnes; " you will not leave me to fhame as well as mifery ?" Clifford promifed every thing fhe wifhed; and Agnes tried to lofe the pangs of parting, in anticipation of the joy of his return. But on the very day that Agnes expected him, fhe received a letter from him, faying that he was under failing orders, and to fee her again before the embarkation was impoffible.

To do Clifford juftice, he in this inftance told truth; and, as he really loved Agnes as well as a libertine can love, he felt the agitation and diftrefs which his letter ex-preffed; though, had he returned to her, he had an excufe ready prepared for delaying the marriage.

Words can but ill defcribe the fituation of Agnes on the receipt of this letter— The return of Clifford was not to be ex-pected of months at leaft; and perhaps he might never return !—The thought of his

danger

danger was madnefs :—but when fhe reflected that fhe fhould in all probability be
a mother before fhe became a wife, fhe
rolled herfelf on the floor in a tranfport of
frantic anguifh, and implored Heaven in
mercy to put an end to her exiftence.—
"O ! my dear, injured father !" fhe exclaimed, " I who was once your pride, am
now your difgrace !—and that child whofe
firft delight it was to look up in your face,
and fee your eyes beaming with fondnefs
on her, can now never dare to meet their
glance again."

But, though Agnes dared not prefume
to write to her father till fhe could fign
herfelf the wife of Clifford, fhe could not
exift without making fome fecret inquiries
concerning his health and fpirits ; and, before he left her, Clifford recommended a
trufty meffenger to her for the purpofe.—
The firft account fhe received was, that
Fitzhenry was well ; the next, that he was
dejected ; the three following, that his fpirits
were

them with will at once gratify their affec-
tions and their pride—What then muft
have been the fenfations of Agnes at a moment fo awful and dangerous as this !—
Agnes, who had no hufband to foothe her
by his anxious inquiries, no relations or
friends to cheer her drooping foul by the
expreffions of fympathy, and whofe child,
inftead of being welcomed by an exulting
family, muft be, as well as its mother, a
ftranger even to its neareft relation !

But, in proportion to her trials, feemed
to be Agnes's power of rifing fuperior to
them ; and, after enduring her fufferings
with a degree of fortitude and calmnefs
that aftonifhed the miftrefs of the houfe,
whom compaffion had induced to attend
on her, fhe gave birth to a lovely boy—
and from that moment, though fhe rarely
finiled, and never faw any one but her
kind landlady, her mind was no longer oppreffed by the deep gloom fhe had before
laboured under ; and when fhe had heard
from

from Clifford, or of her father's being happy, and clasped her babe to her bosom, Agnes might almost be pronounced cheerful.

After she had been six months a mother, Clifford returned, and in the transport of seeing him safe, Agnes almost forgot she had been anxious and unhappy. Now again was the subject of the marriage resumed; but just as the wedding-day was fixed, Clifford was summoned away to attend his expiring father, and again was Agnes doomed to the tortures of suspense.

After a month's absence Clifford returned, but appeared to labour under a dejection of spirits, which he seemed studious to conceal from her. Alarmed and terrified at an appearance so unusual, she demanded an explanation, which the consummate deceiver gave at length, after many entreaties on her part, and feigned reluctance on his. He told her his father's illness was occasioned by his having been informed that he was privately mar-

ried

ried to her, and that he had sent for him to inquire into the truth of the report; and being convinced by his solemn affurance that no marriage had taken place, he had commanded him, unless he wished to kill him, to take a solemn oath never to marry Agnes Fitzhenry without his consent.

"And did you take the oath?" cried Agnes, her whole frame trembling with agitation.—" What could I do?" replied he; " my father's life in evident danger if I refused;- besides the dreadful certainty that he would put his threats in execution of curfing me with his dying breath;—and, cruel as he is, Agnes, I could not help feeling he was my father."—" Barbarian!" exclaimed she, " I facrificed my father to you!—An oath! O God! have you then taken an oath never to be mine?" and, saying this, she fell into a long and deep swoon.

When she recovered, but before she was able to speak, she found Clifford kneeling

by

by her; and, while she was too weak to
interrupt him, he convinced her that he
did not at all despair of his father's consent
to his making her his wife, else, he should
have been less willing to give so ready a
consent to take the oath imposed on him,
even although his father's life depended on
it. "Oh! no," replied Agnes, with a bitter
smile, "you wrong yourself; you are too
good a son to have been capable of hesi-
tating a moment;—there are few children
so bad, so very bad as I am :"—and, bursting into an agony of grief, it was long before the affectionate language and tender
caresses of Clifford could restore her to
tranquillity.

Another six months elapsed, during which
time Clifford kept her hopes alive, by telling
her he every day saw fresh signs of his father's relenting in her favour :—" At these
times, lead me to him," she would say,
" let him hear the tale of my wretchedness;
let me say to him, For your son's sake I have
left the best of fathers, the happiest of

homes,

homes, and have become an outcaſt from ſo-
ciety; then would I bid him look at this pale
cheek, this emaciated form, proofs of the
anguiſh that is undermining my conſtitu-
tion ; and tell him to beware how, by
forcing you to withhold from me my right,
he made you guilty of murdering the poor
deluded wretch, who, till ſhe knew you,
never lay down without a father's bleſſing,
or roſe but to be welcomed by his ſmile !"

Clifford had feeling, but it was of that
tranſient ſort which never outlived the diſ-
appearance of the objeCt that occaſioned it.
To theſe pathetic entreaties he always returned affeCtionate anſwers, and was often
forced to leave the room in order to avoid
being too much ſoftened by them ; but, by
the time he had reached the end of the
ſtreet, always alive to the impreſſions of
the preſent moment, the ſight of ſome new
beauty, or ſome old companion, dried up the
ſtarting tear, and reſtored to him the power
of coolly conſidering how he ſhould continue to deceive his miſerable viCtim.

But

But the time at length arrived when the mask that hid his villainy from her eyes fell off, never to be replaced. As Agnes fully expected to be the wife of Clifford, she was particularly careful to lead a retired life, and not to seem unmindful of her shame, by exhibiting herself at places of public amusement. In vain did Clifford paint to her the charms of the play, the opera, and other places of fashionable resort. "Retirement, with books, music, work, and your society," she used to reply, "are better suited to my taste and situation; and never, but as your wife, will I presume to meet the public eye."

Clifford, though he wished to exhibit his lovely conquest to the world, was obliged to submit to her will in this instance. Sometimes, indeed, Agnes was prevailed on to admit to her table those young men of Clifford's acquaintance who were the most distinguished for their talents and decorum of manners; but this was the only departure he had ever yet prevailed on her

to

to make, from the plan of retirement she had adopted.

One evening, however, Clifford was so unusually urgent with her to accompany him to Drury-lane to see a favourite tragedy, (urging, as an additional motive for her obliging him, that he was going to leave her on the following Monday, in order to attend his father into the country, where he should be forced to remain some time,) that Agnes, unwilling to refuse what he called his parting request, at length complied; Clifford having prevailed on Mrs. Askew, the kind landlady, to accompany them, and having assured Agnes, that, as they should sit in the upper boxes, she might, if she chose it, wear her veil down. —Agnes, in spite of herself, was delighted with the representation—but, as

—" hearts refin'd the sadden'd tint retain,
" The sigh is pleasure, and the jest is pain,"

she was desirous of leaving the house before the farce began ; yet, as Clifford saw a gen-

a gentleman in the lower boxes with whom
he had bufinefs, fhe confented to fay till
he had fpoken to him.   Soon after fhe faw
Clifford enter the lower box oppofite to
her; and thofe who know what it is to love,
will not be furprifed to hear that Agnes
had more pleafure in looking at her lover,
and drawing favourable comparifons between him and the gentlemen who furrounded him, than in attending to the
farce ; and fhe had been fome moments
abforbed in this pleafing employment when
two gentlemen entered the box where fhe
was, and feated themfelves behind her.

" Who is that elegant, fafhionable-look-
ing man, my lord, in the lower box juft
oppofite to us?" faid one of the gentlemen
to the other—" I mean he who is fpeaking
to Captain Mowbray. — " It is George
Clifford, of the Guards," replied his lordfhip, " and one of the clevereft fellows in
England, colonel."

Agnes, who had not miffed one word of

this

this converfation, now became ftill more attentive.

"O! I have heard a great deal of him," returned the colonel, "and as much againft him as for him."—"Moft likely," faid his lordfhip; "for it is a common remark, that if his heart were not as bad as his head is good, he would be an honour to human nature; but I dare fay that fellow has ruined more young men, and feduced more young women, than any man of his age (which is only four-and-thirty) in the kingdom."

Agnes fighed deeply, and felt herfelf attacked by a fort of faint ficknefs.

"But it is to be hoped he will reform now," obferved the colonel: "I hear he is going to be married to mifs Sandford, the great city heirefs."—"So he is—and Monday is the day fixed for the wedding."

Agnes ftarted:—Clifford himfelf had told her he muft leave her on Monday for fome weeks;—and, in breathlefs expectation, fhe liftened to what followed.

—"But

—" But what then ?" continued his lordſhip ; " he marries for money merely. The truth is, his father is lately come to a long diſputed barony, and with ſcarcely an acre of land to ſupport the dignity of it—ſo his ſon has conſented to marry an heireſs, in order to make the family rich, as well as noble. You muſt know, I have my information from the fountain head — Clifford's mother is my relation, and the good woman thought proper to acquaint me in form with the *advantageous* alliance her hopeful ſon was about to make."

This *confirmation* of the truth of a ſtory, which ſhe till now hoped might be mere report, was more than Agnes could well ſupport ; but, made courageous by deſperation, ſhe reſolved to liſten while they continued to talk on this ſubjeſt. Mrs. Aſkew, in the mean while, was leaning over the box, too much engroſſed by the farce to attend to what was paſſing behind her.——Juſt as his lordſhip concluded the

c 6   laſt

laft fentence, Agnes faw Clifford go out
with his friend ; and fhe who had but the
minute before gazed on him with looks of
admiring fondnefs, now wifhed, in the bitternefs of her foul, that fhe might never behold him again !

"I never wifh," faid the colonel, "a
match of intereft to be a happy one."—
"Nor will this be fo, depend on it," anfwered his lordfhip ; "for, befides that
mifs Sandford is ugly and difagreeable, fhe
has a formidable rival."—"Indeed !" cried
the other ;—"a favourite miftrefs, I fuppofe."

Here the breath of Agnes grew fhorter
and fhorter ; fhe fufpected they were going
to talk of her ; and, under other circumftances, her nice fenfe of honour would
have prevented her attending to a converfation which fhe was certain was not meant
for her ear : but fo great was the importance
of the prefent difcourfe to her future peace
and well-being, that it annihilated all fenfe
of impropriety in liftening to it.

"Yes,

" Yes, he has a favourite miftrefs,"
anfwered his lordfhip—" a girl who was
worthy a better fate."—" You know her,
then ?" afked the colonel.—" No," replied he, " by name only ; but when I
was in the neighbourhood of the town
where fhe lived, I heard continually of her
beauty and accomplifhments : her name is
Agnes Fitz— Fitz—"—" Fitzhenry, I
fuppofe," faid the other.—" Yes, that is the
name," faid his lordfhip ; " how came you
to guefs it ?"—" Becaufe Agnes Fitzhenry
is a name I have often heard toafted : fhe
fings well, does fhe not ?"—" She does
every thing well," rejoined the other ;
" and was once the pride of her father, and
the town fhe lived in."

Agnes could fcarcely forbear groaning
aloud at this faithful picture of what fhe
once was.

" Poor thing !" refumed his lordfhip—
" that ever fhe fhould be the victim of a villain ! It feems he feduced her from her
father's houfe, under pretence of carrying
her

her to Gretna-green; but, on fome infernal plea or another, he took her to London."

Here the agitation of Agnes became fo vifible as to attract Mrs. Afkew's notice; but as fhe affured her fhe fhould be well prefently, Mrs. Afkew again gave herfelf up to the illufion of the fcene. Little did his lordfhip think how feverely he was wounding the peace of one for whom he felt fuch compaffion.

" You feem much interefted about this unhappy girl," faid the colonel.—" I am fo," replied he, " and full of the fubject too; for Clifford's factotum, Wilfon, has been with me this morning, and I learnt from him fome of his mafter's tricks, which made me ftill more anxious about his victim.—It feems fhe is very fond of her father, though fhe was prevailed on to defert him, and has never known a happy moment fince her elopement, nor could fhe be eafy without making frequent but fecret inquiries concerning his health."— " Strange inconfiftency!" muttered the colonel.—

colonel. — " This anxiety gave Clifford room to fear that fhe might at fome future moment, if difcontented with him, return to her afflicted parent before he was tired of her—fo what do you think he did?"—

At this moment Agnes, far more eager to hear what followed than the colonel, turned round, and, fixing her eyes on his lordfhip with wild anxiety, could fcarcely help faying, What did Clifford do, my lord?

—" He got his factotum, the man I mentioned, to perfonate a meffenger, and to pretend to have been to her native town, and then he gave her fuch accounts as were beft calculated to calm her anxiety; but the mafter-ftroke which fecured her remaining with him was, his telling the pretended meffenger to inform her that her father was *married again* — though it is more likely, poor unhappy man, that he is dead, than that he is married."

At the mention of this horrible proba-bility, Agnes loft all felf-command, and, fcreaming aloud, fell back on the knees of

his

his aftonifhed lordfhip, reiterating her cries with all the alarming helpleffnefs of phrenfy.

" Turn her out ! turn her out !" echoed through the houfe—for the audience fup-pofed the noife proceeded from fome in-toxicated and abandoned woman ; and a man in the next box ftruck Agnes a blow on the fhoulder, and, calling her by a name too grofs to repeat, defired her to leave the houfe, and act her drunken freaks elfe-where.

Agnes, whom the gentlemen behind were fupporting with great kindnefs and compaffion, heard nothing of this fpeech, fave the injurious epithet applied to her-felf; and alive only to what fhe thought the juftice of it, " Did you hear that ?" fhe ex-claimed, ftarting from his lordfhip's fup-porting hand, who with the other was col-laring the intoxicated brute that had in-fulted her—" Did you hear that ?—O ! God ! my brain is on fire !"— Then, fpring-ing over the feat, fhe rufhed out of the
box,

box, followed by the trembling and aſto-niſhed Mrs. Aſkew, who in vain tried to keep pace with the deſperate ſpeed of Agnes.

Before Agnes, with all her haſte, could reach the bottom of the ſtairs, the farce ended, and the lobbies began to fill. Agnes preſſed forward, when, amongſt the crowd, ſhe ſaw a tradeſman who lived near her father's houſe.—No longer ſenſible of ſhame, for anguiſh had annihilated it, ſhe ruſhed towards him, and, ſeizing his arm, exclaimed, " For the love of God, tell me how my father is !" The tradeſman, ter-rified and aſtoniſhed at the pallid wildneſs of her look, ſo unlike the countenance of ſucceſsful and contented vice he would have expected to ſee her wear, replied,—" He is well, poor ſoul ! but——"—" But unhappy, I ſuppoſe ?" interrupted Agnes :—" Thank God he is well—but is he married ?"—" Married !—dear me, no ; he is——"—" Do you think he would for-give me ?" eagerly rejoined Agnes. —" Forgive

"Forgive you!" anfwered the man—"How you talk! Belike he might forgive you, if ——."—"I know what you would fay," interrupted Agnes again, "if I would return.—Enough—enough—God blefs you! you have faved me from diftraction."—So faying, fhe ran out of the houfe : Mrs. Afkew having overtaken her, followed by the nobleman and the colonel, who with the greateft confternation had found, from an exclamation of Mrs. Afkew's, that the object of their compaffion was mifs Fitzhenry herfelf!

What the confequence of his lordfhip's addreffing Agnes might have been, cannot be known : whether he would have offered her the protection of a friend, if fhe wifhed to leave Clifford, or whether fhe would have accepted it, muft remain uncertain ; but before he could overtake her, Clifford met her, on his return from a neighbouring coffee-houfe with his companion; and, fpite of her ftruggles and reproaches, which aftonifhed and alarmed him, he, with Mrs.

Afkew's

Afkew's affiftance, forced her into a hack-
ney-coach, and ordered the man to drive
home.—No explanation took place during
the ride. `To all the careffes and queftions
of Clifford, fhe returned nothing but `paf-
fionate exclamations againft his perfidy and
cruelty. Mrs. Afkew thought her infane ;
Clifford wifhed to think her fo ; but his
confcience told him that, if by accident
his conduct had been difcovered to her,
there was reafon enough for the frantic
forrow he witneffed.

At length they reached their lodgings,
which were in Suffolk-ftreet, Charing-
crofs ;. and Agnes, having at length obtained fome compofure, in as few words as
poffible related the converfation fhe had
overheard. Clifford, as might be expected,
denied the truth of what his lordfhip had
advanced; but it was no longer in his power
to deceive the at laft awakened penetra-
tion of Agnes.—Under his affumed uncon-
cern, fhe clearly faw the confufion of de-
tected guilt ; and, giving utterance in very
strong

ſtrong language to the contempt and indignation ſuch complete depravity occaſioned her to feel, ſhe provoked Clifford,
who was more than half intoxicated, boldly
to avow what he was at firſt eager to deny;
and Agnes, who before ſhuddered at his
hypocriſy, was now ſhocked at his unprin-
cipled daring.

"But what right have you to complain?"
added he; "the cheat I put upon you relative to your father, was certainly meant
in kindneſs; and though miſs Sandford
will have my hand, you alone will ever
poſſeſs my heart; therefore it was my de-
ſign to keep you in ignorance of my marriage, and retain you as the greateſt of all
my worldly treaſures. — Plague on his
prating lordſhip! he has deſtroyed the
prettieſt arrangement ever made. However, I hope we ſhall part as good friends
as ever."

"Great God!" cried Agnes, raiſing her
tearleſs eyes to heaven — "is it for a
wretch like *this* I have forſaken the beſt of
parents!

parents!—But think not, fir," fhe added, turning with a commanding air towards Clifford, whofe temper, naturally warm, the term ' wretch ' had not foothed, " think not, fallen as I am, that I will ever condefcend to receive protection and fupport, either for myfelf or child, from a man whom I know to be a confummate villain. You have made me criminal, but you have not obliterated my horror for crime, and my veneration for virtue—and, in the fulnefs of my contempt, I inform you, fir, that we fhall meet no more."

" Not till to-morrow," faid Clifford :— " this is our firft quarrel, Agnes ; and the quarrels of lovers are only the renewal of love, you know ; therefore, leaving this bitter, piercing air to guard my treafure for me till to-morrow, I take my leave, and hope in the morning to find you in better humour."

" So faying, he departed, fecure, from the inclemency of the weather and darknefs of the night, that Agnes would not

venture

venture to go away before the morning, and refolved to return very early in order to prevent her departure, if her threatened refolution were any thing more than the frantic expreffions of a difappointed wo-man. Befides, he knew that at that time fhe was fcantily fupplied with money, and that Mrs. Afkew dared not furnifh her with any for the purpofe of leaving him.

But he left not Agnes, as he fuppofed, to vent her fenfe of injury in idle grief and inactive lamentation, but to think, to de-cide, and to act.——And they, indeed, met no more.——What was the rigour of the night to a woman whofe heart was torn by all the pangs which convictions, fuch as thofe fhe had lately received, could give ? And haftily wrapping up her fleeping boy in a péliffe, which in a calmer moment fhe would have felt the want of herfelf, fhe took him in her arms ; then, throwing a fhawl over her fhoulders, fofily unbarred the hall door, and before the noife could have fummoned any of the family fhe was

already

already out of fight. So fevere was the weather, that even thofe accuftomed to brave in ragged garments the pelting of the pitilefs ftorm, fhuddered as the freezing wind whiftled around them, and crept with trembling knees to the wretched hovel that awaited them. But the winter's wind blew unfelt by Agnes ; fhe was alive to nothing but the joy of having efcaped from a villain, and the faint hope that fhe was haftening to obtain, perhaps, a father's forgivenefs.

" Thank Heaven !" fhe exclaimed, as fhe found herfelf at the rails along the Green Park—" the air which I breathe here is uncontaminated by his breath !" when, as the watchman called paft eleven o'clock, the recollection that fhe had no place of fhelter for the night occurred to her, and at the fame inftant fhe remembered that a coach fet off at twelve from the White Horfe in Piccadilly, that went within twelve miles of her native place. She immediately refolved to haften thither, and, either in the infide or the outfide, to

8   proceed

proceed on her journey as far as her finances would admit of, intending to walk the rest of the way. She arrived at the inn juft as the coach was fetting off, and found, to her great fatisfaction, one infide place vacant.

Nothing worth mentioning occurred on the journey. Agnes with her veil drawn over her face, and holding her flumbering boy in her arms, while the inceffant fhaking of her knee and the piteous manner in which fhe fighed gave evident marks of the agitation of her mind, might excite in fome degree the curiofity of her fellow-travellers, but gave no promife of that curiofity being fatisfied, and fhe was fuffered to remain unquefiioned and unnoticed. At noon the next day the coach ftopped for the travellers to dine, and flay a few hours to recruit themfelves after their labours paft, and fortify themfelves againft thofe yet to come. Here Agnes, who as fhe approached nearer home became afraid of meeting fome acquaintance, refolved to change her drefs, and

and to equip herfelf in fuch a manner as
fhould, while it fkreened her from the inclemency of the weather, at the fame time
prevent her being recognized by any one.
Accordingly fhe exchanged her péliffe,
fhawl, and a few other things, for a man's
great coat, a red cloth cloak with a hood
to it, a pair of thick fhoes, and fome yards
of flannel in which fhe wrapt up her little
Edward; and, having tied her ftraw bonnet
under her chin with her veil, fhe would
have looked like a country woman dreffed
for market, could fhe have divefted herfelf
of a certain delicacy of appearance and
gracefulnefs of manner, the yet uninjured
beauties of former days. But when they
fet off again fhe became an outfide paffenger, as fhe could not afford to continue
an infide one ; and covering her child up
in the red cloak which fhe wore over her
coat, fhe took her ftation on the top of the
coach with feeming firmnefs, but a breaking heart.

Agnes expected to arrive within twelve
miles

miles of her native place long before it was dark, and reach the place of her destination before bed-time, unknown and unseen; but she was mistaken in her expectations, for the roads had been rendered so rugged by the frost, that it was late in the evening when the coach reached the spot whence Agnes was to commence her walk; and by the time she had eaten her slight repast, and furnished herself with some necessaries to enable her to resist the severity of the weather, she found it was impossible for her to reach her long-forsaken home before day-break.

Still she was resolved to go on :—to pass another day in suspense concerning her father, and her future hopes of his pardon, was more formidable to her than the terrors of undertaking a lonely and painful walk. Perhaps, too, Agnes was not sorry to have a tale of hardship to narrate on her arrival at the house of her nurse, whom she meant to employ as mediator between her and her offended parent.

His

His child, his penitent child, whom he had brought up with the utmost tenderness, and skreened with unremitting care from the ills of life, returning, to implore his pity and forgiveness, on foot, and unprotected, through all the dangers of trackless paths, and through the horrors of a winter's night, must, she flattered herself, be a picture too affecting for Fitzhenry to think upon without some commiseration; and she hoped he would in time bestow on her his *forgiveness*;—to be admitted to his presence was a favour which she dared not presume either to ask or expect.

But, in spite of the soothing expectation which she tried to encourage, a dread of she knew not what took possession of her mind.— Every moment she looked fearfully around her, and, as she beheld the wintery waste spreading on every side, she felt awe-struck at the desolateness of her situation. The sound of a human voice would, she thought, have been rapture to her ear, but the next minute she believed it would have made

her

her fink in terror to the ground.—"Alas!"
fhe mournfully exclaimed, " 1 was not always timid and irritable as I now feel—but
then I was not always guilty :—O ! my
child ! would I were once more innocent,
like thee !" then, in a paroxyfm of grief,
fhe bounded forward on her way, as if
hoping to efcape by fpeed from the mifery
of recollection.

Agnes was now arrived at the beginning
of a foreft, about two miles in length, and
within three of her native place. Even in
her happieft days fhe never entered its fo-
lemn fhade without feeling a fenfation of
fearful awe ; but now that fhe entered it,
leaflefs as it was, a wandering wretched
outcaft, a mother without the facred name
of wife, and bearing in her arms the pledge
of her infamy, her knees fmote each other,
and, fhuddering as if danger were before
her, fhe audibly implored the protection of
Heaven.

At this inftant fhe heard a noife, and
cafting a ftartled glance into the obfcurity
before

before her, she thought she saw something
like a human form running across the road.
For a few moments she was motionless with
terror; but, judging from the swiftness with
which the object disappeared that she had
inspired as much terror as she felt, she
ventured to pursue her course : she had not
gone far when she again beheld the cause of
her fear; but, hearing as it moved a noise
like the clanking of a chain, she concluded
it was some poor animal that had been
turned out to graze.

Still, as she gained on the object before
her, she was convinced it was a man she
beheld; and as she heard the noise no
longer, she concluded it had been the result of fancy only; but that, with every
other idea, was wholly absorbed in terror
when she saw the figure standing still, as
if waiting for her approach.—" Yet why
should I fear?" she inwardly observed : " it
may be a poor wanderer like myself, who
is desirous of a companion—if so, I shall
rejoice in such a rencontre."

As

As this reflection paſſed her mind, ſhe
baſtened towards the ſtranger, when ſhe
ſaw him look haſtily round him, ſtart, as if
he beheld at a diſtance ſome object that
alarmed him, and then, without taking
any notice of her, run on as faſt as before.
But what can expreſs the horror of Agnes
when ſhe again heard the clanking of
the chain, and diſcovered that it hung to
the ankle of the ſtranger !—" Sure he muſt
be a felon," murmured Agnes :—" O ! my
poor boy ! perhaps we ſhall both be mur-
dered !—This ſuſpenſe is not to be borne ;
I will follow him, and meet my fate at
once."—Then, ſummoning all her remaining ſtrength, ſhe followed the alarming
fugitive.

After ſhe had walked nearly a mile further, and, as ſhe did not overtake him, had
flattered herſelf he had gone in a contrary
direction, ſhe ſaw him ſeated on the ground,
and, as before, turning his head back with
a ſort of convulſive quickneſs ; but as it
was turned from her, ſhe was convinced
ſhe

she was not the object he was seeking. Of
her he took no notice ; and her resolution of accosting him failing when she approached, she walked hastily past, in hopes
she might escape him entirely. As she
passed she heard him talking and laughing
to himself, and thence concluded he was
not a felon, but a *lunatic* escaped from con-
finement. Horrible as this idea was, her
fear was so far overcome by pity, that she
had a wish to return, and offer him some
of the refreshment which she had procured
for herself and child, when she heard him
following her very fast, and was convinced
by the sound, the dreadful sound of his
chain, that he was coming up to her.

The clanking of a fetter, when one
knows it is fastened round the limbs of a
fellow-creature, always calls forth in the
soul of sensibility a sensation of horror; what
then, at this moment, must have been its
effect on Agnes, who was trembling for her
life, for that of her child, and looking in vain
for a protector round the still, solemn waste!

Breathless

Breathlefs with apprehenfion Agnes ftopped
as the maniac gained upon her, and, motionlefs and fpeechlefs, awaited the confequence of his approach.

"Woman!" faid he, in a hoarfe, hollow tone—"Woman! do you fee them?
do you fee them?"—"Sir! pray what did
you fay, fir?" cried Agnes, in a tone of
refpect, and curtfying as fhe fpoke—for
what is fo refpectful as fear?—"I can't fee
them," refumed he, not attending to her,
"I have efcaped them! Rafcals! cowards!
I have efcaped them!" and then he jumped
and clapped his hands for joy.

Agnes, relieved in fome meafure from
her fears, and eager to gain the poor
wretch's favour, told him fhe rejoiced at
his efcape from the rafcals, and hoped they
would not overtake him: but while fhe
fpoke he feemed wholly inattentive, and,
jumping as he walked, made his fetter
clank in horrid exultation.—The noife at
length awoke the child, who, feeing a
ftrange object before him, and hearing a
                                        found

found fo unufual, fcreamed violently, and hid his face in his mother's bofom.

"Take it away! take it away!" exclaimed the maniac—"I do not like children."—And Agnes, terrified at the thought of what might happen, tried to foothe the trembling boy to reft, but in vain; the child ftill fcreamed, and the angry agitation of the maniac increafed.—"Strangle it! ftrangle it!" he cried—"do it this moment, or——" Agnes, almoft frantic with terror, conjured the unconfcious boy, if he valued his life, to ceafe his cries; and then the next moment fhe conjured the wretched man to fpare her child: but, alas! fhe fpoke to thofe incapable of underftanding her—a child and a madman! —The terrified boy ftill fhrieked, the lunatic ftill threatened, and, clenching his fift, feized the left arm of Agnes, who with the other attempted to defend her infant from his fury; when, at the very moment that his fate feemed inevitable, a fudden gale of wind fhook the leaflefs

D 5

branches

branches of the furrounding trees, and the madman, fancying the noife proceeded from his purfuers, ran off with the rapidity of lightning.

Immediately, the child, relieved from the fight and the found which alarmed it, and exhaufted by the violence of its cries, funk into a found fleep on the throbbing bofom of its mother. — But, alas! Agnes knew this was but a temporary efcape — the maniac might return, and again the child might wake in terrors; and fcarcely had the thought paffed her mind, when fhe faw him returning; but, as he walked flowly, the noife was not fo great as before.

" I hate to hear children cry," faid he, as he approached.——" Mine is quiet now," replied Agnes; then, recollecting fhe had fome food in her pocket, fhe offered fome to the ftranger in order to divert his attention from the child. He fnatched it from her hand inftantly, and devoured it with terrible voracioufnefs: but again he exclaimed,

claimed, " I do not like children ; if you truſt them they will betray you :" and Agnes offered him food again, as if to bribe him to ſpare her helpleſs boy.—" I had a child once—but ſhe is dead, poor ſoul !" continued he, taking Agnes by the arm, and leading her gently forward.—" And you loved her very tenderly, I ſuppoſe ?" ſaid Agnes, thinking the loſs of his child had occaſioned his malady ; but, inſtead of anſwering her, he went on :—" They ſaid ſhe ran away from me with a lover—but I knew they lied — ſhe was good, and would not have deſerted the father who doted on her—Beſides, I ſaw her funeral myſelf—Liars, raſcals, as they are!—do not tell any one, I got away from them laſt night, and am now going to viſit her grave."

A death-like ſickneſs, an apprehenſion ſo horrible as to deprive her almoſt of ſenſe, took poſſeſſion of the ſoul of Agnes. She eagerly endeavoured to obtain a ſight of the ſtranger's face, but in vain, as his

hat

hat was pulled over his forehead, and his chin rested on his bosom. They had now nearly gained the end of the forest, and day was just breaking : Agnes, as soon as they entered the open plain, seized the arm of the madman to force him to look towards her—for speak to him she could not. He felt, and perhaps resented the importunate pressure of her hand—for he turned hastily round—when, dreadful confirmation of her fears, Agnes beheld her father ! ! !

It was indeed Fitzhenry, driven to madness by his daughter's desertion and disgrace ! !

After the elopement of Agnes, Fitzhenry entirely neglected his business, and thought and talked of nothing but the misery he experienced. In vain did his friends represent to him the necessity of his making amends, by increased diligence, for some alarming losses in trade which he had lately sustained. She, for whom alone he toiled, had deserted him—and ruin had no

terrors

terrors for him.——" I was too proud of her," he ufed mournfully to repeat——" and Heaven has humbled me even in her by whom I offended."

Month after month elapfed, and no intelligence of Agnes.——Fitzhenry's dejection increafed, and his affairs became more and more involved : at length, abfolute and irretrievable bankruptcy was become his portion, when he learnt from authority not to be doubted, that Agnes was living with Clifford as his acknowledged miftrefs.—— This was the death-ftroke to his reafon ; and the only way in which his friends (relations he had none, or only diftant ones) could be of any further fervice to him was, by procuring him admiffion into a private madhoufe in the neighbourhood.

Of his recovery little hope was entertained.——The conftant theme of his ravings was his daughter ;——fometimes he bewailed her as dead ; at other times he complained of her as ungrateful :—but fo complete was the overthrow his reafon had received,
                                                            that

that he knew no one, and took no notice of those whom friendfhip or curiofity led to his cell : yet he was always meditating his efcape; and though ironed in confequence of it, the night he met Agnes he had, after incredible difficulty and danger, effected his purpofe.

But to return to Agnes—who, when fhe beheld in her infane companion her injured father, the victim probably of her guilt, let fall her fleeping child, and, finking on the ground, extended her arms towards Fitz-henry, articulating in a faint voice, " O God ! my father !" then proftrating her-felf at his feet, fhe clafped his knees in an agony too great for utterance.

At the name of " father," the poor ma-niac ftarted, and gazed on her earneftly, with favage wildnefs, while his whole frame became convulfed ; and rudely difengaging himfelf from her embrace, he ran from her a few paces, and then dafhed himfelf on the ground in all the violence of phrenfy. He raved, he tore his hair ; he fcreamed,

and

and uttered the moſt dreadful execrations ; and with his teeth ſhut and his hands clenched, he repeated the word father, and ſaid the name was mockery to him.

Agnes, in mute and tearful deſpair, beheld the dreadful ſcene ; in vain did her affrighted child cling to her gown, and in its half formed accents entreat to be taken to her arms again ; ſhe ſaw, ſhe heeded nothing but her father ; ſhe was alive to nothing but her own guilt and its conſequences ; and ſhe awaited with horrid compoſure the ceſſation of Fitzhenry's phrenſy, or the direction of its fury towards her child.

At laſt, ſhe ſaw him fall down exhauſted and motionleſs, and tried to haſten to him ; but ſhe was unable to move, and reaſon and life ſeemed at once forſaking her, when Fitzhenry ſuddenly ſtarted up, and approached her.—Uncertain as to his purpoſe, Agnes caught her child to her boſom, and, falling again on her knees, turned on him her almoſt cloſing eyes ; but his countenance was mild—and gently patting

4   her

her forehead, on which hung the damps of approaching infenfibility, " Poor thing !" he cried, in a tone of the utmoft tendernefs and compaffion, " Poor thing !" and then gazed on her with fuch inquiring and mournful looks, that tears once more found their way and relieved her burfting brain—while feizing her father's hand fhe preffed it with frantic emotion to her lips.

Fitzhenry looked at her with great kindnefs, and fuffered her to hold his hand— then exclaimed, " Poor thing !—don't cry —don't cry—I can't cry—I have not cried for many years ; not fince my child died— for fhe is dead, is fhe not ?" looking earneftly at Agnes, who could only anfwer by her tears.—" Come," faid he, " come," taking hold of her arm, then laughing wildly, " Poor thing ! you will not leave me, will you ?"—"Leave you !" fhe replied, " never :—I will live with you—die with you."—" True, true," cried he, " fhe is dead, and we will go vifit her grave."—So, faying, he dragged Agnes forward with great

great velocity; but as it was along the path leading to the town, she made no resistance.

Indeed it was such a pleasure to her to see that though he knew her not, the sight of her was welcome to her unhappy parent, that she sought to avoid thinking of the future, and to be alive only to the present; she tried also to forget that it was to his not knowing her she owed the looks of tenderness and pity he bestowed on her, and that the hand which now kindly held hers would, if recollection returned, throw her from him with just indignation.

But she was soon awakened to redoubled anguish, by hearing Fitzhenry, as he looked behind him, exclaim, " They are coming, they are coming :" and as he said this, he ran with frantic haste across the common. Agnes immediately looking behind her, saw three men pursuing her father at full speed, and concluded that they were the keepers of the bedlam whence he had escaped.

efcaped. Soon after fhe faw the poor
lunatic coming towards her, and had
fcarcely time to lay her child gently on
the ground, before Fitzhenry threw himfelf in her arms, and implored her to fave
him from his purfuers.

In an agony that mocks defcription,
Agnes clafped him to her heart, and
awaited in trembling agitation the approach of the keepers.——" Hear me, hear
me," fhe cried, " I conjure you to leave
him to my care :—He is my father, and
you may fafely truft him with me."——
" Your father !" replied one of the men ;
" and what then, child ? You could do
nothing for him, and you fhould be thank-
ful to us, young woman, for taking him
off your hands.—So come along, mafter,
come along," he continued, feizing Fitzhenry, who could with difficulty be fepa-
rated from Agnes——while another of the
keepers, laughing as he beheld her wild
anguifh, faid, " We fhall have the daughter

as

as well as the father foon, I fee, for I
do not believe there is a pin to choofe between them."

But, fevere as the fufferings of Agnes
were already, a ftill greater pang awaited
her. The keepers finding it a very difficult tafk to confine Fitzhenry, threw him
down, and tried by blows to terrify him
into acquiefcence. At this outrage Agnes
became frantic indeed, and followed them
with fhrieks, entreaties, and reproaches ;
while the ftruggling victim called on her
to protect him, as they bore him by violence along, till, exhaufted with anguifh
and fatigue, fhe fell infenfible on the
ground, and loft in a deep fwoon the confcioufnefs of her mifery.

How long fhe remained fo is uncertain ;
but when fhe recovered her fenfes all was
ftill around her, and fhe miffed her child.
—Starting up, and looking round with
renewed phrenfy, fhe faw it lying at fome
diftance from her, and on taking it up fhe
found it in a deep fleep. The horrid apprehenfion

prehension immediately rushed on her mind, that such a sleep in the midst of cold so severe was the sure forerunner of death.

"Monster!" she exclaimed, "destroyer of thy child, as well as father!——But perhaps it is not yet too late, and my curse is not completed."——So saying, she ran, or rather flew, along the road; and seeing a house at a distance she made towards it, and, bursting open the door, beheld a cottager and his family at breakfast——then, sinking on her knees, and holding out to the woman of the house her sleeping boy, "For the love of God," she cried, "look here! look here! Save him! O! save him!" A mother appealing to the heart of a mother is rarely unsuccessful in her appeal.——The cottager's wife was as eager to begin the recovery of the child of Agnes as Agnes herself, and in a moment the whole family was employed in its service; nor was it long before they were rewarded for their humanity by its complete restoration.

The joy of Agnes was frantic as her grief

grief had been.——She embraced them all
by turns, in a loud voice invoked bleffings on their heads, and promifed, if fhe
was ever rich, to make their fortune :——
laftly, fhe caught the ftill languid boy to
her heart, and almoft drowned it in her
tears.

In the cottager and his family a fcene
like this excited wonder as well as emotion.
He and his wife were good parents——they
loved their children —— would have been
anxious during their illnefs, and would
have forrowed for their lofs : but to thefe
violent expreffions and actions, the refult
of cultivated fenfibility, they were wholly
unaccuftomed, and could fcarcely help
imputing them to infanity——an idea which
the pale cheek and wild look of Agnes
ftrongly confirmed ; nor did it lofe ftrength
when Agnes, who in terror at her child's
danger and joy for his fafety had forgotten
even her father and his fituation, fuddenly
recollecting herfelf, exclaimed, " Have I
dared to rejoice ?——Wretch that I am! Oh!
no——

no—there is no joy for me!" The cottager and his wife, on hearing these words,
looked significantly at each other.

Agnes soon after started up, and, clasp-
ing her hands, cried out, "O! my father,
my dear, dear father! thou art past cure;
and despair must be my portion."

"O! you are unhappy because your
father is ill," observed the cottager's wife;
"but do not be so sorrowful on that account,
he may get better perhaps."—"Never,
never," replied Agnes; "yet, who knows?"
—"Aye — who knows indeed," resumed
the good woman. "But if not, you nurse
him yourself, I suppose, and it will be a
comfort to you to know he has every thing
done for him that can be done."—Agnes
sighed deeply.—"I lost my own father,"
continued she, "last winter, and a hard
trial it was, to be sure; but then it con-
soled me to think I made his end comfort-
able. Besides, my conscience told me, that,
except here and there, I had always done
my duty by him, to the best of my knowledge."

ledge." Agnes ftarted from her feat, and walked rapidly round the room. "He finiled on me," refumed her kind hoftefs, wiping her eyes, "to the laft moment; and juft before the breath left him, he, faid, 'Good child, good child.'—O! it muft be a terrible thing to lofe one's parents when one has not done one's duty to them."

At thefe words Agnes, contrafting her conduct and feelings with thofe of this artlefs and innocent woman, was overcome with defpair, and, feizing a knife that lay by her, endeavoured to put an end to her exiftence; but the cottager caught her hand in time to prevent the blow, and his wife eafily difarmed her, as her violence inftantly changed into a fort of ftupor; then throwing herfelf back on the bed on which fhe was fitting, fhe lay with her eyes fixed, and incapable of moving.

The cottager and his wife now broke forth into expreffions of wonder and horror at the crime fhe was going to commit, and

and the latter, taking little Edward from
the lap of her daughter, held it towards
Agnes—" See," cried fhe, as the child
ftretched forth its little arms to embrace
her—" unnatural mother! would you forfake your child ?"

Thefe words, affifted by the careffes of
the child himfelf, roufed Agnes from her
ftupor. — " Forfake him! Never, never !"
fhe faltered out, and, fnatching him to
her bofom, threw herfelf back on a pillow
the good woman had placed under her
head; and foon, to the great joy of the compaffionate family, both mother and child
fell into a found fleep. The cottager then
repaired to his daily labour, and his wife
and children began their houfehold tafks;
but ever and anon they caft a watchful
glance on their unhappy gueft, dreading
left fhe fhould make a fecond attempt on
her life.

The fleep of both Agnes and her child
was fo long and heavy, that night was
clofing in when the little boy awoke, and

by

by his cries for food, broke the reft of his unhappy mother.

But confcioufnefs returned not with returning fenfe—Agnes looked around her, aftonifhed at her fituation. At length, by flow degrees, the dreadful fcenes of the preceding night, and her own rafh attempt, burft on her recollection; fhe fhuddered at the retrofpect, and, clafping her hands together, remained for fome moments in fpeechlefs prayer:—then fhe arofe; and fmiling mournfully at fight of her little Edward eating voracioufly the milk and bread that was fet before him, fhe feated herfelf at the table, and tried to partake of the coarfe but wholefome food provided for her. As fhe approached, fhe faw the cottager's wife remove the knives, and leave a fork and fpoon only for her to eat with. This circumftance forcibly recalled her rafh action, and drove away her returning appetite.—" You may truft me now," fhe faid; " I fhrink with horror from my wicked attempt on my life, and

E   fwear,

ſwear, in the face of Heaven, never to repeat it; no—my only wiſh now is, to live
and to ſuffer."

Soon after, the cottager's wife made an
excuſe for bringing back a knife to the
table, to prove to Agnes her confidence in
her word; but this well-meant attention
was loſt on her—ſhe ſat leaning on her elbow, and wholly abſorbed in her own me-
ditations.

When it was completely night, Agnes
aroſe to depart.—" My kind friends," ſaid
ſhe, " who have ſo hoſpitably received and
entertained a wretched wanderer, believe
me I ſhall never forget the obligations I
owe you, though I can never hope to repay
them; but accept this (taking her laſt half-
guinea from her pocket) as a pledge of my
inclination to reward your kindneſs. If I
am ever rich again—" Here her voice
failed her, and ſhe burſt into tears.

This heſitation gave the virtuous people
ſhe addreſſed an opportunity of rejecting
her offers.—" What we did, we did becaufe

caufe we could not help it," faid the cottager—"You would not have had me fee a fellow-creature going to kill foul and body too, and not prevent it, would you?" —" And as to faving the child," cried the wife, "am I not a mother myfelf, and can I help feeling for a mother? Poor little thing! it looked, fo piteous too, and felt fo cold!"

Agnes could not fpeak; but ftill, by figns, fhe tendered the money to their acceptance.—"No, no," refumed the cottager, "keep it for thofe who may not be willing to do you a fervice for nothing;"— and Agnes reluctantly replaced the half-guinea. But then a frefh fource of altercation began; the cottager infifted on feeing Agnes to the town, and fhe infifted on going by herfelf: at laft fhe agreed he fhould go with her as far as the ftreet where her friends lived, wait for her at the end of it, and if they were not living, or were removed, fhe was to return, and fleep at the cottage.

Then, with a beating heart and dejected countenance, Agnes took her child

in

in her arms, and, leaning on her companion, with flow and unsteady steps she began her walk to her native place, once the scene of her happiness and her glory, but now about to be the witness of her misery and her shame.

As they drew near the town, Agnes saw, on one side of the road, a new building, and instantly hurried from it as fast as her trembling limbs could carry her.— " Did you hear them ?" asked the cottager. —" Hear whom ?" said Agnes.—" The poor creatures," returned her companion, " who are confined there.—That is the new bedlam—and hark ! What a loud scream that was !"—Agnes, unable to support herself, staggered to a bench that projected from the court surrounding the building, while the cottager, unconscious why she stopped, observed it was strange she should like to stay and hear the poor creatures —For his part he thought it shocking to hear them shriek, and still more so to hear them laugh—" for it is so piteous," said he, " to hear those laugh who have so much reason to cry."

Agnes

Agnes had not power to interrupt him, and he went on :—" This houfe was built by fubfcription ; and it was begun by a kind gentleman of the name of Fitzhenry, who afterwards, poor foul, being made low in the world by loffes in trade, and by having his brain turned by a good-for-nothing daughter, was one of the firft patients in it himfelf."—Here Agnes, to whom this recollection had but too forcibly occurred already, groaned aloud.—" What, tired fo foon ?" faid her companion . " I doubt you have not been ufed to ftir about —you have been too tenderly brought up. Ah! tender parents often fpoil children, and they never thank them for it when they grow up neither, and often come to no good befides."

Agnes was going to make fome obfervation, wrung from her by the poignancy of felf-upbraiding, when fhe heard a loud cry as of one in agony ; and fancying it her father's voice, fhe ftarted up, and, ftopping

E 3   her

her ears, ran towards the town fo faft that it was with difficulty that the cottager could overtake her. When he did fo, he was furprifed at the agitation of her manner.——" What, I fuppofe you thought they were coming after you?" faid he. " But there was no danger—I dare fay it was only an unruly one whom they were beating."—Agnes, on hearing this, abfolutely fcreamed with agony; and, feizing the cottager's arm, " Let us haften to the town," faid fhe in a hollow and broken voice, " while I have ftrength enough left to carry me thither."

At length they entered its walls, and the cottager faid, " Here we are at laft.—A welcome home to you, young woman."— " Welcome! and home to me!" cried Agnes wildly—" I have no home now—I can expect no welcome! Once indeed——" Here, overcome with recollections almoft too painful to be endured, fhe turned from him and fobbed aloud, while the

kind-

kind-hearted man could fcarcely forbear
fhedding tears at fight of fuch myfterious,
yet evidently real diftrefs.

In happier days, when Agnes ufed to
leave home on vifits to her diftant friends,
anticipation of the welcome fhe fhould
receive on her return was, perhaps, the
greateft pleafure fhe enjoyed during her
abfence. As the adventurer to India, while
toiling for wealth, never lofes fight of the
hope that he fhall fpend his fortune in his
native land; fo Agnes, whatever company
fhe faw, whatever amufements fhe partook
of, looked eagerly forward to the hour
when fhe fhould give her expecting father,
and her affectionate companions, a recital
of all fhe had heard and feen. For, though
fhe had been abfent a few weeks only,
" her prefence made a little holiday," and
fhe was received by Fitzhenry with delight too deep to be expreffed; while,
even earlier than decorum warranted, her
friends were thronging to her door to welcome home the heightener of their plea-

E 4   fures,

fures, and the gentle foother of their forrows ; (for Agnes " loved and felt for all :"
fhe had a fmile ready to greet the child of
profperity, and a tear for the child of adverfity)—As fhe was thus honoured, thus
beloved, no wonder the thoughts of home,
and of returning home, were wont to
fuffufe the eyes of Agnes with tears of exquifite pleafure ; and that, when her native
town appeared in view, a group of expecting and joyful faces ufed to fwim before her
fight, while, haftening forward to have the
firft glance of her, fancy ufed to picture
her father !———Now, dread reverfe ! after a
long abfence, an abfence of years, fhe was
returning to the fame place, inhabited by
the fame friends : but the voices that ufed
to be loud in pronouncing her welcome,
would now be loud in proclaiming indignation at her fight ; the eyes that ufed to
beam with gladnefs at her prefence, would
now be turned from her with difguft ; and
the fond father, who ufed to be counting
the moments till fhe arrived, was now———

I fhall

I fhall not go on——fuffice, that Agnes
felt, to " her heart's core," all the bitternefs
of the contraft.

When they arrived near the place of
her deftination, Agnes ftopped, and told
the cottager that they muft part.——" So
much the worfe," faid the good man. " I
do not know how it is, but you are fo forrowful, yet fo kind and gentle, fomehow,
that both my wife and I have taken a lik-
ing to you :—you muft not be angry, but
we cannot help thinking you are not one
of us, but a lady, though you are fo dif-
guifed and fo humble—but misfortune
fpares no one, you know."

Agnes, affected and gratified by thefe
artlefs expreffions of good will, replied,
—" I have, indeed, known better days"—
" And will again, I hope with all my
heart and foul," interrupted the cottager
with great warmth.——" I fear not," replied Agnes, " my dear worthy friend."—
" Nay, young lady," rejoined he, " my
wife and I are proper to be your fervants,

not

not friends."—" You are my friends, perhaps my only friends," returned Agnes mournfully: " perhaps there is not, at this moment, another hand in the universe that would not reject mine, or another tongue that would not upbraid me."—" They must be hard-hearted wretches, indeed, who could upbraid a poor woman for her misfortunes," cried the cottager: " however, you shall never want a friend while I live. You know I saved your life; and, somehow, I feel now as if you belonged to me. I once saved one of my pigeons from a hawk, and I believe, were I starving, I could not now bear to kill the little creature; it would seem like eating my own flesh and blood—so I am sure I could never desert you."—" You have not yet heard my story," replied Agnes; " but you shall know who I am soon, and then, if you still feel disposed to offer me your friendship, I shall be proud to accept it."

The house to which Agnes was hastening was that of her nurse, from whom she

had

had always experienced the affection of a
mother, and hoped now to receive a temporary afylum ; but fhe might not be living—and, with a beating heart, Agnes
knocked at the door. It was opened by
Fanny, her nurfe's daughter, the playfel-
low of Agnes's childhood.—" Thank Heaven!" faid Agnes, as fhe haftened back to
the cottager, " I hope I have, at leaft, one
friend left ;" and telling him he might go
home again, as fhe was almoft certain of
fhelter for the night; the poor man fhook
her heartily by the hand, prayed God to
blefs her, and departed.

Agnes then returned to Fanny, who was
fiill flanding by the door, wondering who
had knocked at fo late an hour, and difpleafed at being kept fo long in the cold—
" Will you admit me, Fanny, and give
me fhelter for the night ?" faid Agnes in
a faint and broken voice.—" Gracious
heaven! who are you ?" cried Fanny, ftarting
back. " Do you not know me ?" fhe replied,
looking earneftly in her face.—Fanny again

E 6   ftarted ;

ſtarted; then burſting into tears, as ſhe drew Agnes forward, and cloſed the door—" O God! it is my dear young lady!"—" And are you ſorry to ſee me?" replied Agnes.—" Sorry!" anſwered the other.—" Oh, no! but to ſee you thus!—O! my dear lady, what you muſt have ſuffered! Thank Heaven my poor mother is not alive to ſee this day!"

" And is ſhe dead?" cried Agnes, turning very faint, and catching hold of a chair to keep her from falling. " Then is the meaſure of my affliction full: I have loſt my oldeſt and beſt friend!"—" I am not dead," ſaid Fanny reſpectfully.—" Excellent, kind creature!" continued Agnes, " I hoped ſo much alleviation of my miſery from her affection!"—" Do you hope none from mine?" rejoined Fanny in a tone of reproach—" Indeed, my dear young lady, I love you as well as my mother did, and will do as much for you as ſhe would have done. Do I not owe all I have to you? and now that you are in trouble,

trouble, perhaps in want too—But no, that cannot and fhall not be," wringing her hands and pacing the room with frantic violence : " I can't bear to think of fuch a thing. That ever I fhould live to fee my dear young lady in want of the help fhe was always fo ready to give!"

Agnes tried to comfort her ; but the fight of her diftrefs notwithftanding was foothing to her, as it convinced her fhe was ftill dear to one pure and affectionate heart.

During this time little Edward remained covered up fo clofely that Fanny did not know what the bundle was that Agnes held in her lap ; but when fhe lifted up the cloak that concealed him, Fanny was in an inftant kneeling by his fide, and gazing on him with admiration—" Is it—is it—" faid Fanny with hefitation—" It is my child," replied Agnes, fighing ; and Fanny lavifhed on the unconfcious boy the careffes which refpect forbade her to beftow on the mother.

" Fanny,"

" Fanny," faid Agnes, " you fay nothing of your hufband ?"—" He is dead,"
replied Fanny with emotion.—" Have you
any children ?"—" None."—" Then will
you promife me, if I die, to be a mother
to this child ?"—Fanny feized her hand,
and, in a voice half choked by fobs, faid, " I
promife you." — "Enough," cried Agnes ;
then holding out her arms to her humble
friend, Fanny's refpect yielded to affection,
and, falling on Agnes's neck, fhe fobbed
aloud.

" My dear Fanny," faid Agnes, " I have
a queftion to afk, and I charge you to anfwer it truly."—" Do not afk me, do not
afk me, for indeed I dare not anfwer you,"
replied Fanny in great agitation. Agnes
gueffed the caufe, and haftened to tell her
that the queftion was not concerning her
father, as fhe was acquainted with his fituation already, and proceeded to afk whether
her elopement and ill conduct had at all
haftened the death of her nurfe, who was

in

in ill health when she went away.——" Oh
no," replied Fanny, " she never believed
that you could be gone off willingly, but
was sure you were spirited away, and she
died expecting you would some day return,
and take the law of the villain ; and no
doubt she was right, though nobody thinks
so now but me, for you were always too
good to do wrong."

Agnes was too honourable to take to
herself the merit she did not deserve : she
therefore owned she was indeed guilty ;
" nor should I," she added, " have dared
to intrude myself on you, or solicit you to
let me remain under your roof, were I not
severely punished for my crime, and resolved to pass the rest of my days in soli-
tude and labour."——" You should not presume to intrude yourself on me !" replied
Fanny——" Do not talk thus, if you do not
mean to break my heart."——"Nay, Fanny,"
answered Agnes, " it would be presump-
tion in any woman who has quitted the
path of virtue to intrude herself, however
high

high her rank might be, on the meaneft of her acquaintance whofe honour is fpotlefs. Nor would I thus throw myfelf on your generofity were I not afraid that, if I were to be unfoothed by the prefence of a fym-pathizing friend, I fhould fink beneath my forrows, and want refolution to fulfil the hard tafk my duty enjoins me."

I fhall not attempt to defcribe the an-guifh of Fanny when fhe thought of her young lady, the pride of her heart, as fhe ufed to call her, being reduced fo low in the world, nor the fudden burfts of joy fhe gave way to the next moment when fhe reflected that Agnes was returned, never perhaps to leave her again.

Agnes wore away great part of the night in telling Fanny her mournful tale, and in hearing from her a full account of her fa-ther's fufferings, bankruptcy, and confe-quent madnefs. At day-break fhe retired to bed, not to fleep, but ruminate on the romantic yet in her eyes feafible plan fhe had formed for the future — while

Fanny,

Fanny, wearied out by the violent emotions she had undergone, sobbed herself to sleep by her side.

The next morning Agnes did not rise till Fanny had been up some time ; and when she seated herself at the breakfast-table, she was surprised to see it spread in a manner which ill accorded with her or Fanny's situation. On asking the reason, Fanny owned she could not bear her dear young lady should fare as she did only, and had therefore provided a suitable breakfast for her.—" But you forget," said Agnes, " that if I remain with you, neither you nor I can afford such breakfasts as these."— " True," replied Fanny mournfully, " then you must consider this as only a welcome, madam."—" Aye," rejoined Agnes, " the prodigal is returned, and you have killed the fatted calf." Fanny burst into tears ; while Agnes, shocked at having excited them by the turn she unguardedly gave to her poor friend's attention, tried to sooth her

her into compofure, and affected a gaiety
which fhe was far from feeling.

"Now then to my firft tafk," faid Agnes,
rifing as foon as fhe had finifhed her breakfaft : "I am going to call on Mr. Seymour ; you fay he lives where he formerly
did."——"To call on Mr. Seymour !" exclaimed Fanny ; "O ! my dear madam, do
not go near him, I befeech you ; he is a
very fevere man, and will affront you, depend upon it."——" No matter," rejoined
Agnes, " I have deferved humiliation, and
will not fhrink from it : but his daughter
Caroline, you know, was once thy deareft
friend, and fhe will not fuffer him to
trample on the fallen ; and it is neceffary I
fhould apply to him in order to fucceed
in my fcheme."——" What fcheme ?" replied Fanny. " You would not approve it,
Fanny, therefore I fhall not explain it to
you at prefent; but, when I return, perhaps
I fhall tell you all."——" But you are not
going fo foon ? not in day-light, furely ?
If you fhould be infulted !"

Agnes

Agnes ftarted with horror at this proof which Fanny had unguardedly given, how hateful her guilt had made her in a place that ufed to echo with her praifes—but, recovering herfelf, fhe faid fhe fhould welcome infults as part of the expiation fhe meant to perform. "But if you will not avoid them for your own fake, pray, pray do for mine," exclaimed Fanny. "If you were to be ill ufed, I am fure I fhould never furvive it : fo, if you muft go to Mr. Seymour's, at leaft oblige me in not going before dark :" and, affected by this frefh mark of her attachment, Agnes confented to ftay.

At fix o'clock in the evening, while the family was fitting round the fire, and Caroline Seymour was expecting the arrival of her lover, to whom fhe was to be united in a few days, Agnes knocked at Mr. Seymour's door, having pofitively forbidden Fanny to accompany her. Caroline, being on the watch for her intended bridegroom, ftarted at the found ; and though the knock

knock Agnes gave did not much refemble
that of an impatient lover, fiill " it might
be he"—" he might mean to furprife her ;"
and, half opening the parlour door, fhe
liftened with a beating heart for the fervant's anfwering the knock.

By this means fhe diftinctly heard Agnes
afk whether Mr. Seymour was at home. The
fervant ftarted, and ftammered out that he
believed his mafter was within — while
Caroline, fpringing forward, exclaimed,
" I know that voice—O yes! it muft be
fhe !"—But her father, feizing her arm,
pufhed her back into the parlour, faying,
" I alfo know that voice, and I command
you to ftay where you are. "—Then going
up to Agnes, he defired her to leave his
houfe directly, as it fhould be no har-
bour for abandoned women and unnatural
children.

" But will you not allow it to fhelter for
one moment the wretched and the penitent ?" fhe replied. " Father, my dear,
dear father," cried Caroline, again coming
forward,

forward, but was again driven back by Mr. Seymour, who, turning to Agnés, bade her claim fhelter from the man for whom fhe had left the beft of parents; and defiring the fervant to fhut the door in her face, he re-entered the parlour, whence Agnes diftinctly heard the fobs of the compaffionate Caroline.

But the fervant was kinder than the mafter, and could not obey the orders he had received.—" O madam ! mifs Fitzhenry, do you not know me ?" faid he. " I once lived with you ; have you forgotten little William ? I fhall never forget you ; you were the fweeteft tempered young lady——That ever I fhould fee you thus !"

Before Agnes could reply, Mr. Seymour again angrily afked why his orders were not obeyed ; and Agnes, checking her emotion, befought William to deliver a meffage to his mafter. " Tell him," faid fhe, " all I afk of him is, that he will ufe

his

his interet to get me the place of fervant in the houfe, the bedlam I would fay, where——he will know what I mean," fhe added, unable to utter the conclufion of the fentence—and. William, in a broken voice, delivered the meffage.

"O my poor Agnes !" cried Caroline paffionately—" A fervant ! fhe a fervant ! and in fuch a place too !" William adding in a low voice—" Ah ! mifs ! and fhe looks fo poor and wretched !"

Meanwhile Mr. Seymour was walking up and down the room hefitating how to act ; but, reflecting that it was eafier to forbid any communication with Agnes than to check it if once begun, he again defired William to fhut the door againft her. "You muft do it yourfelf then," replied William, " for I am not hard-hearted enough ;"—and Mr. Seymour, fummoning up refolution, told Agnes there were other governors to whom fhe might apply, and then locked the door againft her himfelf—
while

while Agnes flowly and forrowfully turned her fteps towards Fanny's more hofpitable roof.

She had not gone far, however, when fhe heard a light footftep behind her, and her name pronounced in a gentle, faltering voice—and turning round fhe beheld Caroline Seymour, who, feizing her hand, forced fomething into it, haftily preffed it to her lips, and, without faying one word, fuddenly difappeared, leaving Agnes motionlefs as a ftatue, and, but for the parcel fhe held in her hand, difpofed to think fhe was dreaming.——Then, eager to fee what it contained, fhe haftened back to Fanny, who heard with indignation the reception fhe had met from Mr. Seymour, but on her knees invoked bleffings on the head of Caroline, when on opening the parcel fhe found it contained twenty guineas inclofed in a paper, on which was written, but almoft effaced with tears, " For my ftill dear Agnes—would I dare fay more !"

4   **This**

This money the generous girl had taken from that allowed her for wedding-clothes, and felt more delight in relieving with it the wants even of a guilty fellow-creature, than purchasing the most splendid dress could have afforded her. And her present did more than she expected; it relieved the mind of Agnes: she had taught herself to meet without repining the assaults of poverty, but not to encounter with calmness the scorn of the friends she loved.

But Caroline and her kindness soon vanished again from her mind, and the idea of her father, and her scheme, took entire possession of it—" But it might not succeed—no doubt Mr. Seymour would be her enemy—still he had hinted she might apply to the other governors;" and Fanny having learnt that they were all to meet at the bedlam on business the next day, she resolved to write a note, requesting to be allowed to appear before them.

This

This note, Fanny, who was not acquainted with its contents, undertook to
deliver, and, to the great furprife of Agnes
(as fhe expected Mr. Seymour would oppofe it), her requeft was inftantly granted.
Indeed it was Mr. Seymour himfelf who
urged the compliance.

There was not a kinder-hearted man in
the world than Mr. Seymour; and in his
feverity towards Agnes he acted more from
what he thought his duty, than from his
inclination. He was the father of feveral
daughters, and it was his opinion a parent
could not too forcibly inculcate on the minds
of young women the falutary truth, that
lofs of virtue muft be to them the lofs of
friends. Befides, his eldeft daughter, Caroline, was going to be married to the fon
of a very fevere, rigid mother, then ftaying
at the houfe, and he feared that, if he took
any notice of the fallen Agnes, the old
lady might conceive a prejudice againft
him and her daughter-in-law. Added to
thefe reafons, Mr. Seymour was a very vain

f   man.

man, and never acted in any way without
saying to himself, " What will the world
say ?" Hence, though his first impulses
were frequently good, the determinations
of his judgment were often contemptible.

But, however satisfied Mr. Seymour
might be with his motives on this occasion,
his feelings revolted at the consciousness
of the anguish he had occasioned Agnes.
He wished, ardently wished; he had dared
to have been kinder: and when Caroline,
who was incapable of the meanness of con-
cealing any action which she thought it
right to perform, told him of the gift she
had in person bestowed on Agnes, he
could scarcely forbear commending her
conduct; and, while he forbade any future
intercourse between them, he was forced
to turn away his head to hide the tear of
gratified sensibility, and the smile of parental exultation : nevertheless, he did
not omit to bid her keep her own coun-
sel, " for, if your conduct were known,"
added he, " what would the world say ?"

No

No wonder then, that, foftened as he was by Agnes's application, though he deemed the fcheme wild and impracticable, and afraid he had treated her unkindly, he was pleafed to have an opportunity of obliging her, without injuring himfelf, and that her requeft to the governors was ftrengthened by his reprefentations; nor is it extraordinary, that, alive as he always was to the opinion of every one, he fhould dread feeing Agnes after the reception he had given her, more than Agnes dreaded to appear before the board.

Agnes, who had borrowed of Fanny the drefs of a refpectable maid fervant, when fummoned to attend the governors, entered the room with modeft but dignified compofure, prepared to expect contumely, but refolved to endure it as became a contrite heart. But no contumely awaited her.

In the hour of her profperity fhe had borne her faculties fo meekly, and had been fo careful never to humble any one

by

by showing a confcioufnefs of fuperiority, that fhe had been beloved even more than fhe had been admired; and hard indeed muft the heart of that man have been, who could have rejoiced that fhe herfelf was humbled.

A dead, nay a folemn filence took place on her entrance. Every one prefent beheld with furprife, and with *ftolen* looks of pity, the ravages which remorfe and anguifh had made in her form, and the ftriking change in her apparel; for every one had often followed with delight her graceful figure through the dance, and gazed with admiration on the tafteful varieties of her drefs; every one had liftened with pleafure to the winning found of her voice, and envied Fitzhenry the poffeffion of fuch a daughter. As they now beheld her, thefe recollections forcibly occurred to them :——they agonized——they overcame them.——They thought of their own daughters, and fecretly prayed Heaven to keep them from the voice of the feducer :——

away

away went all their refolutions to receive
Agnes with that open difdain and detef-
tation which her crime deferved ; the
fight of her difarmed them ; and not one
amongft them had, for fome moments,
firmnefs enough to fpeak.   At laft, " Pray
fit down, mifs Fitzhenry," faid the prefident in a voice hoarfe with emotion :
" Here is a chair," added another ; and
Mr. Seymour, bowing as he did it, placed
a feat for her near the fire.

Agnes, who had made up her mind to
bear expected indignity .with compofure,
was not proof againft unexpected kindnefs ;
and, haftily turning to the window, fhe
gave vent to her fenfations in an agony of
tears.   But, recollecting the importance
of the bufinefs on which fhe came, fhe
ftruggled with her feelings ; and on being
defired by the prefident to explain to the
board what fhe wanted, fhe began to addrefs
them in a faint and faltering voice : however,
as fhe proceeded, fhe gained courage, re-
membering it was her intereft to affect her

auditors,

auditors, and make them enter warmly into her feelings and defigns. She told her whole ftory, in as concife a manner as poffible, from the time of her leaving Clifford to her rencontre with her father in the foreft, and his being torn from her by the keepers; and when fhe was unable to go on, from the violence of her emotions, fhe had the fatisfaction of feeing that the tears of her auditors kept pace with her own. When her narrative was ended, fhe proceeded thus :———

"I come now, gentlemen, to the reafon of my troubling you. From the impreffion the fight of me made on my father, I feel a certain conviction that, were I conftantly with him, I might in time be able to re-ftore to him that reafon my guilt has de-prived him of. To effect this purpofe, it is my wifh to become a fervant in this houfe: if I fhould not fucceed in my endeavours, I am fo fure he will have pleafure in feeing me, that I feel it my duty to be with him, even on that account ; and,

and, if there be any balm for a heart and
confcience fo wounded as mine, I muft find
it in devoting all my future days to alleviate, though I cannot cure, the mifery I
have occafioned. And if," added fhe with
affecting enthufiafm, " it fhould pleafe
Heaven to fmile on my endeavours to
reftore him to reafon, how exquifite will
be my fatisfaction in labouring to maintain him !"

To this plan, it is to be fuppofed, the
governors faw more objection than Agnes
did ; but, though they rejected the idea of
her being a fervant in the houfe, they were
not averfe to giving her an opportunity
of making the trial fhe defired, if it were
only to alleviate her evident wretchednefs ;
and, having confulted the medical attendants belonging to the inftitution, they
ordered that Agnes fhould be permitted
two hours at a time, morning and evening,
to fee Fitzhenry. And fhe, who had not
dared to flatter herfelf fhe fhould obtain
fo much, was too full of emotion to fhow,

F 4   otherwife

otherwife than by incoherent expreffions and broken fentences, her fenfe of the obligation.

" Our next care", obferved the prefident, " muft be, as friends of your poor father, to fee what we can do for your future fupport."—" That, fir, I fhall provide for myfelf," replied Agnes; " I will not eat the bread of idlenefs, as well as of fhame and affliction, and fhall even rejoice in being obliged to labour for my fupport, and that of my child—happy, if, in ful- filling well the duties of a mother, I may make fome atonement for having violated thofe of a daughter."

" But, mifs Fitzhenry," anfwered the prefident, " accept at leaft fome affiftance from us till you can find means of main- taining yourfelf."—" Never, never," cried Agnes : " I thank you for your kindnefs, but I will not accept it ; nor do I need it. I have already accepted affiftance from one kind friend, and merely becaufe I fhould, under fimilar circumftances, have been

hurt

hurt at having a gift of mine refufed ; but, allow me to fay that, from the wretched-nefs into which my guilt has plunged me, nothing henceforward but my induftry fhall relieve me."

So faying, fhe curtfied to the gentlemen, and haftily withdrew, leaving them all deeply affected by her narrative, and her propofed expiatory plan of life, and ready to grant her their admiration, fhould fhe have refolution to fulfil her good intentions, after the ftrong impreffion which the meeting with her father in the foreft had made on her mind, fhould have been weakened by time and occupation.

Agnes haftened from the governors' room to put in force the leave fhe had obtained, and was immediately conducted to Fitzhenry's cell. She found him with his back to the door, drawing with a piece of coal on the wall ; and as he did not ob-ferve her entrance, fhe had an opportunity of looking over his fhoulder, and fhe faw that he had drawn the fhape of a coffin,

F 5   and

and was then writing on the lid the name of Agnes.

A groan which involuntarily escaped her made him turn round; at sight of her he started, and looked wildly as he had done in the forest; then, shaking his head and sighing deeply, he resumed his employment, still occasionally looking back at Agnes; who, at length overcome by her feelings, threw herself on the bed beside him, and burst into tears.

Hearing her sobs, he immediately turned round again, and, patting her check as he had done on their first meeting, said, " Poor thing ! poor thing !" and, fixing his eyes stedfastly on her face, while Agnes turned towards him and pressed his hand to her lips, he gazed on her as before with a look of anxious curiosity ; then, turning from her, muttered to himself, " She is dead, for all that."

Soon after, he asked her to take a walk with him ; adding, in a whisper, " We will go find her grave ;" and, taking her under

under his arm, he led her to the garden, smiling on her from time to time, as if it gave him pleasure to see her; and sometimes laughing, as if at some secret satisfaction which he would not communicate. When they had made one turn round the garden, he suddenly stopped, and began singing—" Tears such as tender fathers shed," that pathetic song of Handel's, which he used to delight to hear Agnes sing : " I can't go on," he observed, looking at Agnes ; " can you ?" as if there were in his mind some association between her and that song ; and Agnes, with a bursting heart, took up the song where he left off.

Fitzhenry listened with restless agitation ; and when she had finished, she desired her to sing it again. " But say the words first," he added : and Agnes repeated——

" Tears such as tender fathers shed,
Warm from my aged eyes descend,
For joy, to think, when I am dead,
My son will have mankind his friend."

P 6

" No

"No, no," cried Fitzhenry with quickness, ' for joy to think when I am dead, Agnes will have mankind her friend.' I used to sing it so; and so she did, when I bade her do so. O! she sung it so well !—But she can sing it no more now, for she is dead; and we will go look for her grave."

Then he ran hastily round the garden, while Agnes, whom the words of this song, by recalling painful recollections, had almost deprived of reason, sat down on a bench, nearly insensible, till he again came to her, and, taking her hand, said, in a hurried manner, "You will not leave me, will you?" And on her answering No, in a very earnest and passionate manner, he looked delighted; and, saying "Poor thing!" again gazed on her intently; and again Agnes's hopes that he would in time know her returned.———" Very pale, very pale!" cried Fitzhenry the next moment, stroking her cheek; " and *she* had such a bloom !—Sing again; for the love of God, sing again :" ——and in a hoarse, broken voice,

voice, Agnes complied. " She fung better than you," rejoined he when fhe had done ;—" fo fweet, fo clear it was !—But fhe is gone !" So faying, he relapfed into total indifference to Agnes, and every thing around him—and again her new-raifed hopes vanifhed.

The keeper now told her it was time for her to depart ; and fhe mournfully arofe ; but, firft feizing her father's hand, fhe leaned for a moment her head on his arm ; then, bidding God blefs him, walked to the door with the keeper. But on feeing her about to leave him, Fitzhenry ran after her, as faft as his heavy irons would let him, wildly exclaiming, " You fhall not go—you fhall not go."

Agnes, overjoyed at this evident proof of the pleafure her prefence gave him, looked at the keeper for permiffion to ftay ; but as he told her it would be againft the rules, fhe thought it more prudent to fubmit ; and before Fitzhenry could catch hold of her in order to detain her by force, fhe she ran through the house, and the grated door was closed on her.

"And this," said Agnes to herself, turning round to survey the melancholy mansion she had left, while mingled sounds of groans, shrieks, shouts, laughter, and the clanking of irons, burst upon her ears, " this is the abode of my father! and provided for him by me!—This is the recompense bestowed on him by the daughter whom he loved and trusted, in return for years of unparalleled fondness and indulgence!"

The recollection was too horrible; and Agnes, calling up all the energy of her mind, remembered the uselessness of regret for the past, but thought with pleasure on the advantages of amendment for the present and the future: and by the time she reached Fanny's door, her mind had recovered its sad composure.

Her countenance, at her return, was very different to what it had been at her departure.

departure. Hope animated her funk eye, and she seemed full of joyful though diftant expectations : nay, so much was she abforbed in pleafing anticipations, that she feebly returned the careffes of her child, who climbed up her knees to exprefs his joy at feeing her ; and even while she kiffed his ruddy cheek, her eye looked beyond it with the open gaze of abfence.

"I have feen him again," she cried, turning to Fanny ; "and he almoft knew me ! He will know me entirely, in time ; and next, he will know every thing ; and then I shall be happy !"

Fanny, to whom Agnes had given no clue to enable her to underftand this language, was alarmed for her intellects, till she explained her plans, and her hopes ; which Fanny, though she could not share in them, was too humane to difcourage.

"But now," continued Agnes, "let us confult on my future means of gaining a livelihood ;" and finding that Fanny, befides keeping a day-fchool, took in fhawl-work,

work, a confiderable fhawl manufacture
being carried on in the town, it was fettled
that fhe fhould procure the fame employment for Agnes; and that a fmall back
room in Fanny's little dwelling fhould be
fitted up for her ufe.

In the mean while the governors of the
bedlam had returned to their refpective
habitations, with feelings towards Agnes
very different to thofe with which they
had affembled. But too prudent to make
even a penitent finner the fubject of praife
in their own families, they gave fhort,
evafive anfwers to the inquiries that were
made there.

Mr. Seymour, on the contrary, thought
it his duty to relieve the generous and affectionate heart of his daughter, by a
minute detail of what had paffed at the
meeting; but he had no opportunity of
doing this when he firft returned home,
as he found there a large party affembled
to dinner. Caroline, however, watched
his countenance and manner; and feeing

4

on the firſt an expreſſion of highly-awak-
ened feelings, and in the latter à degree
of abſence, and averſion to talking, which
it always diſplayed whenever his heart had
been deeply intereſted, ſhe flattered herſelf that Agnes was the cauſe of theſe
appearances, and hoped to hear of ſome-
thing to her advantage.

During dinner, a lady aſked Caroline
which of her young friends would accompany her to church, in the capacity of
bride-maid. Caroline ſtarted, and turned
pale at the queſtion—for melancholy were
the reflections it excited in her mind. It
had always been an agreement between her
and Agnes, that whichever of the two was
married firſt ſhould have the other for her
bride maid ; and the queſtion was repeated
before Caroline could truſt her voice to
anſwer it. " I ſhall have no bride-maids,
but my fiſters," ſhe replied at length with
a quivering lip : " I cannot ; indeed I wiſh
to have no other now." Then, looking at
her father, ſhe ſaw his eyes were filled
with

with tears; and unable to fupprefs, but wifhing to conceal his emotion, he abruptly left the room.

There is fcarcely any human being whofe heart has not taught him that we are never fo compaffionate and benevolent towards others, as when our own wifhes are completely gratified—we are never fo humble as then. This was the cafe with Mr. Seymour; he was about to marry his eldeft daughter in a manner even fuperior to his warmeft expectations, and his paternal care, therefore, was amply rewarded. But his heart told him that his care and his affection had not exceeded, perhaps not equalled, that of Fitzhenry; nor had the promife of his daughter's youth, fair as it was, ever equalled that of the unhappy Agnes; yet Caroline was going to aggrandize her family, and Agnes had difgraced hers. Shé was happy—, Agnes miferable. He was the poffeffor of a large fortune, and all the comforts of life; and Fitzhenry was in a madhoufe.

This

This contrast between their situations was forcibly recalled to his mind by the question addressed to Caroline; and already softened by the interview of the morning, he could not support his feelings, but was obliged to hasten to his chamber to vent in tears and thankfgivings the mingled sensations of humility and gratitude. Caroline soon followed him; and heard, with emotions as violent, her father's description of Agnes's narration, and her conduct before the governors.

" But it is not sufficient," said she, " that you tell me this : you must tell it wherever you hear the poor penitent's name mentioned, and avow the change it has made in your sentiments towards her; you must be her advocate."

" Her advocate ! What would the world say ?"

" Just what you wish it to say. Believe me, my dear father, the world is in many instances like a spoiled child, who treats with contempt the foolish parent that indulges

dulges his caprices, but behaves with refpect to thofe, who, regardlefs of his cla-
mours, give the law to him, inftead of
receiving it."

~ " You fpeak from the untaught enthufiafm and confidence of youth, Caroline—but experience will teach you that
no one can with impunity run counter to
the opinions of the world."

" My experience has taught me that
already ; but, in this cafe, you do not feem
to do the world juftice. The world would
blame you, and juftly too, if, while talking of the unhappy Agnes, you fhould
make light of her guilt ; but why not,
while you acknowledge that to be enormous, defcant with equal juftice on the
deep fenfe fhe entertains of it, and on the
excellence of her prefent intentions ? To
this, what can the world fay, but that you
are a juft judge ? And even fuppofe they
fhould think you too lenient a one, will
not the approbation of your own confcience
be an ample confolation for fuch a con-
demnation ?

demnation ? O ! my dear father ! were you not one of the beſt, and moſt *unſpoilable* of men, your anxious attention to what the world will ſay of your actions, muſt long ere this have made you one of the worſt."

" Enough, enough," cried Mr. Seymour, wounded ſelf-love contending in his boſom with parental pride, for he had ſome ſuſpicion that Caroline was right, " what would the world ſay, if it were to hear you ſchooling your father ?"

" When the world hears me trying to exalt my own wiſdom by doubting my father's, I hope it will treat me with the ſeverity I ſhall deſerve."

Mr. Seymour claſped her to his boſom as ſhe ſaid this, and involuntarily exclaimed, " O ! poor Fitzhenry !"—" And poor Agnes too!" retorted Caroline, throwing her arms round his neck : " it will be my parting requeſt, when I leave my paternal roof, that you will do all the juſtice you can to my once-honoured friend— and

and let the world fay what it pleafes."—
" Well, well, I will indulge you, by
granting your requeft," cried Mr. Seymour; " or rather, I will indulge myfelf."
And then, contented with each other, they
returned to the company.

A few days after this converfation Caroline's marriage took place, and was celebrated by the ringing of bells and other
rejoicings. " What are the bells ringing
for to-day?" faid Agnes to Fanny, as fhe
was eating her breakfaft with more appetite than ufual. Fanny hefitated; and
then, in a peevifh tone, replied, that fhe
fuppofed they rang for mifs Caroline Seymour, as fhe was married that morning:—
adding, " Such a fufs indeed! fuch preparations! one would think nobody was
ever married before!"

Yet, fpitefully as Fanny fpoke this, fhe
had no diflike to the amiable Caroline;
her pettifhnefs proceeded merely from her
love for Agnes. Juft fuch preparations,
juft fuch rejoicings, fhe had hoped to fee

one

one day for the marriage of her dear young lady;—and though Agnes had not perceived it, Fanny had for the laft two days fhed many a tear of regret and mortification, while news of the intended wedding reached her ear on every fide : and fhe had not courage to tell Agnes what fhe heard, left the feelings of Agnes on the occafion fhould refemble hers, but in a more painful degree. "Caroline Seymour married !" cried Agnes, rifing from her unfinifhed meal ; "well married, I hope ?"—"O yes, very well indeed—Mr. Seymour is fo proud of the connection !" "Thank God-!" faid Agnes fervently ; "May fhe be as happy as her virtues deferve !"—and then with a hafty ftep fhe retired to her own apartment.

It is certain that Agnes had a mind above the meannefs of envy, and that fhe did not repine at the happinefs of her friend ; yet, while with tears trickling down her cheek fhe faltered out the words "Happy Caroline !—Mr. Seymour proud !

Well

Well may he be fo!" her feelings were as bitter as thofe which envy excites. "O! my poor father! I once hoped—" added fhe; but overcome with the acutenefs of regret and remorfe, fhe threw herfelf on the bed in fpeechlefs anguifh.

Then the image of Caroline, as fhe laft faw her, weeping for her misfortunes, and adminiftering to her wants, recurred to her mind, and, in a tranfport of affection and gratitude, fhe took the paper that contained the gift from her bofom, kiffed the blotted fcrawl on the back of it, and prayed fervently for her happinefs.

"But furely," cried fhe, ftarting up, and running into the next room to Fanny, "I fhould write a few lines of congratulation to the bride?" Fanny did not anfwer; indeed fhe could not; for the affectionate creature was drowned in tears, which Agnes well underftood, and was gratified, though pained, to behold. At length, ftill more afhamed of her own weaknefs when fhe faw it reflected in another,

another, Agnes gently reproved Fanny, telling her it seemed as if she repined at mifs Seymour's happinefs.

"No," replied Fanny, "I only repine at your mifery. Dear me, fhe is a fweet young lady, to be fure, but no more to be compared to you———"——"Hufh! Fanny; 'tis I who am now not to be compared to her;——remember, my mifery is owing to my guilt."——"It is not the lefs to be repined at on that account," replied Fanny.

To this remark, unconfcioufly fevere, Agnes with a figh affented, and, unable to continue the converfation in this ftrain, fhe again afked whether Fanny did not think fhe ought to congratulate the generous Caroline. "By all means," replied Fanny: but, before fhe anfwered, Agnes had determined that it would be kinder in her not to damp the joy of Caroline, by calling to her mind the image of a wretched friend. "True," fhe obferved; "it would gratify my feelings to exprefs the love and

G   gratitude

gratitude I bear her, and my felf-love would exult in being recollected by her with tenderneſs and regret, even in the hour of her bridal fplendour ; but the gratification would only be a felfiſh one, and therefore I will rejeĉt it."

Having formed this laudable refolution, Agnes, after trying to compofe her agitated fpirits by playing with her child, who was already idoliſed by the faithful Fanny, bent her fteps as ufual to the cell of her father. Unfortunately for Agnes, ſhe was obliged to paſs the houſe of Mr. Seymour, and at the door ſhe faw the carriages waiting to convey the bride and her train to the country feat of her mother-in-law. Agnes hurried on as faſt as her trembling limbs could carry her : but, as ſhe caſt a haſty glance on the fplendid liveries, and the crowd gazing on them, ſhe faw Mr. Seymour buſtling at the door, with all the pleaſed confequence of a happy parent in his countenance ; and not daring to analyſe her feelings, ſhe ruſhed forward

6

from

from the mirthful fcene, and did not ſtop again till ſhe found herſelf at the door of the bedlam.

But when there, and when, looking up at its grated windows, ſhe contemplated it as the habitation of her father—ſo different to that of the father of Caroline—and beheld in fancy the woe-worn, ſallow face of Fitzhenry, ſo unlike the healthy, ſatisfied look of Mr. Seymour—" I can't go in, I can't ſee him to-day," ſhe faintly articulated, overcome with a ſudden faintneſs—and, as ſoon as ſhe could recover her ſtrength, ſhe returned home ; and, ſhutting herſelf up in her own apartment, ſpent the reſt of the day in that mournful and ſolitary meditation that " maketh the heart better."

It would no doubt have gladdened the heart of the poor mourner to have known, that, ſurrounded by joyous and congratulating friends, Caroline ſighed for the abſent Agnes, and felt the want of her congratulations.—" Surely ſhe will write to me !"

me!" said she mentally, " I am sure she wishes me happy ! and one of my greatest pangs at leaving my native place is, the consciousness that I leave her miserable."

The last words that Caroline uttered, as she bade adieu to the domestics, were, " Be sure to send after me any note or letter that may come." But no note or letter from Agnes arrived ; and had Caroline known the reason, she would have loved her once happy friend the more.

The next day, earlier than usual, Agnes went in quest of her father. She did not absolutely flatter herself that he had missed her the day before, still she did not think it absolutely *impossible* that he *might*. She dared not, however, ask the question ; but, luckily for her, the keeper told her, un-asked, that Fitzhenry was observed to be restless, and looking out of the door of his cell frequently, both morning and evening, as if expecting somebody ; and that, at night, as he was going to bed, he asked whether the lady had not been there.

" Indeed !"

" Indeed !" cried Agnes, her eyes sparkling with pleafure – " Where is he ?—Let me fee him directly." But, after the firft joyful emotion which he always fhowed at feeing her had fubfided, fhe could not flatter herfelf that his fymptoms were more favourable than before.

The keeper alfo informed her that he had been thrown into fo violent a raving fit, by the agitation he felt at parting with her the laft time fhe was there, that fhe muft contrive to flip away unperceived whenever fhe came : and this vifit having paffed away without any thing material occurring, Agnes contrived to make her efcape unfeen.

On her return fhe repeated to Fanny feveral times, with a fort of pathetic pleafure, the queftion her father had afked—" He inquired whether the lady had not been there ; — think of that, Fanny :" while fo incoherent was her language and fo abfent were her looks, that Fanny again

began

began to fear her afflictions had impaired her reason.

After staying a few days with the new-married couple, Mr. Seymour returned home, Caroline having before he left her again desired him to be the friend of the penitent Agnes, whenever he heard her unpityingly attacked ; and an opportunity soon offered of gratifying his daughter's benevolence, and his own.

Mr. Seymour was drinking tea in a large party, when a lady, to whose plain, awkward, uninteresting daughters, the once beautiful, graceful, and engaging Agnes had formerly been a powerful rival, said, with no small share of malignity, " So !—fine impudence indeed !—I hear that good for nothing minx, Fitzhenry's daughter, is come to town : I wonder for my part she dares show her face here——But the assurance of those creatures is amazing."

" Aye, it is indeed," echoed from one lady

lady to another. "But this girl muſt be a hardened wretch indeed," reſumed Mrs. Macfiendy, the firſt ſpeaker. "I ſuppoſe her fellow is tired of her, and ſhe will be on the town ſoon——"

"In the church-yard rather," replied Mr. Seymour, whom a feeling of reſentment at theſe vulgar expreſſions of female ſpite had hitherto kept ſilent :—— "Miſs Fitzhenry has loſt all power of charming the eye of the libertine, and even the wiſh ;—but ſhe is an objeċt whom the compaſſionate and humane cannot behold, or liſten to, without the ſtrongeſt emotion."

"No, to be ſure," replied Mrs. Macfiendy bridling——"the girl had always a plauſible tongue of her own——and as to her beauty, I never thought that was made for laſting.——What then you have ſeen her, Mr. Seymour ? I wonder you could condeſcend to *look* at ſuch traſh."

"Yes, madam, I have ſeen, and heard her too ;——and if heartfelt miſery, contri-

tion,

tion, and true penitence, may hope to win favour in the fight of God, and expiate paft offences, ' a miniftering angel might this frail one be, though we lay howling.' "

" I lie howling, indeed !" fcreamed out Mrs. Macfiendy : " fpeak for yourfelf, if you pleafe, Mr. Seymour ; for my part, I do not expect when I go to another world to keep fuch company as mifs Fitzhenry."

" If with the fame meafure you mete it fhould be meted to you again, madam, I believe there is little chance in another world that you and mifs Fitzhenry will be vifiting acquaintance." Then, befpeaking the attention of the company, he gave that account of Agnes, her prefent fitua-tion, and her intentions for the future, which fhe gave the governors ; and all the company, fave the outrageoufly virtuous mother and her daughters, heard it with as much emotion as Mr. Seymour felt in relating it.—Exclamations of " Poor un-fortunate girl ! what a pity fhe fhould

have

have been guilty!—But, fallen as she is, she is still Agnes Fitzhenry," resounded through the room.

Mrs. Macfiendy could not bear this in silence; but, with a cheek pale, nay livid, with malignity, and in a voice sharpened by passion, which at all times resembled the scream of a pea-hen, she exclaimed, "Well, for my part, some people may do any thing, yet be praised up to the skies; other people's daughters would not find such mercy. Before she went off, it was miss Fitzhenry this, and miss Fitzhenry that,—though other people's children could perhaps do as much, though they were not so fond of showing what they could do."

"No," cried one of the miss Macfiendys, "miss Fitzhenry had courage enough for any thing."

"True, child," resumed the mother; "and what did it end in? Why, in becoming a——what I do not choose to name."

"Fie,

" Fie, madam, fie," cried Mr. Seymour; " why thus exult over the fallen ?"

" O ! then you do allow her to be fallen ?"

" She is fallen indeed, madam," faid Mr. Seymour ; " but, even in her proudeft hour, mifs Fitzhenry never expreffed herfelf towards her erring neighbours with un-chriftian feverity ;—but fet you an example of forbearance, which you would do well to follow."

" She fet *me* an example !" vociferated Mrs. Macfiendy—" fhe indeed ! a-crea-ture !—I will not ftay, nor fhall my daugh-ters, to hear fuch immoral talk. But 'tis as I faid—fome people may do any thing —for, wicked as fhe is, mifs Fitzhenry is ftill cried up as fomething extraordinary, and is even held up as an example to modeft women."

So faying, fhe arofe ; but Mr. Seymour rofe alfo, and faid, " There is no neceffity for *your* leaving the company, madam, as I will leave it, for I am tired of hearing
myfelf

myfelf fo grofsly mifreprefented. No one
abhors more than I do the crime of mifs
Fitzhenry; and no one would more ftrongly
object, for the fake of other young women,
to her being again received into general
company; but, at the fame time, I will
always be ready to encourage the penitent
by the voice of juft praife; and I feel
delight in reflecting that, however the
judges of this world may be fond of condemning her, fhe will one day appeal from
them to a merciful and long-fuffering
judge."

Then, bowing refpectfully to all but
Mrs. Macfiendy, he withdrew, and gave
her an opportunity of remarking that Mr.
Seymour was mighty warm in the creature's defence. She did not know he was
fo interefted about her; but fhe always
thought him *a gay man*, and fhe fuppofed
mifs Fitzhenry, as he called her, would be
glad to take up with any thing *now*.

This fpeech, forry am I to fay, was received with a general and complaifant finile,

though

though it was reckoned unjuſt; for there are few who have virtue and reſolution enough to ſtand forward as champions for an abſent and calumniated individual, if there bè any thing ludicrous in the tale againſt him;—and the preciſe, careful, elderly Mr. Seymour, who was always ſhrinking, like a ſenſitive plant, from the touch of cenſure, accuſed by implication of being the private friend of the youthful Agnes, excited a degree of merry malice in the company not unpleaſant to their feelings.

But, in ſpite of the efforts of calumny, the account Mr. Seymour had given of Agnes and her penitence became town talk; and, as it was confirmed by the other governors, every one, except the ferociouſly chaſte, was eager to prevent Agnes from feeling pecuniary diſtreſs, by procuring her employment.

Still ſhe was not ſupplied with work as faſt as ſhe executed it; for, except during the hours which ſhe was allowed to ſpend

with

with her father, she was constantly employed ; and she even deprived herself of
her usual quantity of sleep, and was never
in bed before one, or after four.

In proportion as her business and profits
increased, were her spirits elevated : but
the more she gained, the more saving she
became : she would scarcely allow herself
sufficient food or clothing ; and, to the
astonishment of Fanny, the once generous
Agnes appeared penurious, and a lover of
money. " What does this change mean,
my dear lady ?" said Fanny to her one
day. " I have my reasons for it," replied
Agnes coldly ; then changed the subject ;
and Fanny respected her too much to urge
an explanation.

But Agnes soon after began to wonder
at an obvious change in Fanny. At first,
when Agnes returned from visiting her
father, Fanny used to examine her countenance ; and she could learn from that,
without asking a single question, whether
Fitzhenry seemed to show any new symptoms

ptoms of amendment, or whether his infanity ftill appeared incurable. If the former, Fanny, tenderly preffing her hand,
would fay, " Thank God !" and prepare
their dinner or fupper with more alacrity
than ufual : if the latter, Fanny would fay
nothing ; but endeavour, by bringing little
Edward to her, or by engaging her in converfation, to divert the gloom fhe could
not remove ; and Agnes, though fhe took
no notice of thefe artlefs proofs of affection, obferved and felt them deeply ; and
as fhe drew near the houfe, fhe always anticipated them as one of the comforts of
her home.

But, for fome days paft, Fanny had dif-
continued this mode of welcome fo grateful to the feelings of Agnes, and feemed
wholly abforbed in her own. She was
filent, referved, and evidently oppreffed
with fome anxiety which fhe was ftudious
to conceal. Once or twice, when Agnes
came home rather fooner than ufual, fhe
found her in tears ; and when fhe affec-
tionately

tionately afked the reafon of them, Fanny
pleaded mere lownefs of fpirits as the
caufe.

But the eye of anxious affection is not
eafily blinded. Agnes was convinced that
Fanny's mifery had fome more important
origin; and, fecretly fearing that it proceeded
from her, fhe was on the watch for fomething to confirm her fufpicions.

One day, as fhe paffed through the room
where Fanny kept her fchool, Agnes obferved that the number of her fcholars
was confiderably diminifhed; and, when
fhe afked Fanny where the children whom
fhe miffed were, there was a confufion
and hefitation in her manner, while fhe
made different excufes for their abfence,
which convinced Agnes that fhe concealed
from her fome unwelcome truth.

A very painful fufpicion immediately
darted acrofs her mind, the truth of which
was but too foon confirmed. A day or two
after, while again paffing through the fchool-
room, fhe was attracted by the beauty of
a little

a little girl, who was about eight years old ;
and, fmoothing down her curling hair, fhe
ftooped to kifs her ruddy cheek ; but the
child, uttering a loud fcream, fprung from
her arms, and, fobbing violently, hid her
face on Fanny's lap. Agnes, who was very
fond of children, was much hurt by fymp-
ptoms of a diflike fo violent towards her,
and urged the child to give a reafon for
fuch ftrange conduct : on which the artlefs girl owned that her mother had charged
her never to touch or go near mifs Fitzhenry, becaufe fhe was the moft wicked
woman that ever breathed.

Agnes heard this new confequence of
her guilt with equal furprife and grief;
but, on looking at Fanny, though fhe faw
grief in her countenance, there was no
furprife in it ; and fhe inftantly told her
fhe was convinced the lofs of her fcholars
was occafioned by her having allowed her
to refide with her. Fanny, burfting into
tears, at laft confeffed that her fufpicions
were juft, while to the fhuddering Agnes

4   fhe

fhe unfolded a feries of perfecutions which fhe had undergone from her employers, becaufe fhe had declared her refolution of ftarving, rather than drive from her houfe her friend and benefactrefs.

Agnes was not long in forming her refolution ; and the next morning, without faying a word to Fanny on the fubject, fhe went out in fearch of a lodging for herfelf and child—as gratitude and juftice forbade her to remain any longer with her perfecuted companion.

But after having in vain tried to procure a lodging fuitable to the low ftate of her finances, or rather to her faving plan, fhe hired a little cottage on the heath above the town, adjoining to that where fhe had been fo hofpitably received in the hour of her diftrefs ; and, having gladdened the hearts of the friendly cottager and his wife by telling them fhe was coming to be their neighbour, fhe went to break the unwelcome tidings to Fanny.

Paffionate and vehement indeed was her
diftrefs

diftrefs at hearing her young lady, as fhe ftill perfifted to call her, was going to leave her; but her expoftulations and tears were vain; and Agnes, after promifing to fee Fanny every day, took poffeffion that very evening of her humble habitation.

But her intention in removing was fruf-trated by the honeft indignation and in-difcretion of Fanny. She loudly raved againft the illiberality which had robbed her of the fociety of all fhe held dear; and, as fhe told every one that Agnes left her by her own choice and not at her defire, thofe children, who had been taken away becaufe Agnes refided with her, were not fent back to her on her removal. At laft, the number of her fcholars became fo fmall, that fhe gave up fchool-keeping, and employed herfelf in fhawl-working only; while her leifure time was fpent in vifiting Agnes, or in inveighing, to thofe who would liften to her, againft the cruelty that had driven her young lady from her houfe.

Fanny

Fanny ufed to begin by relating the many obligations her mother and fhe had received from Agnes and her father, and always ended with faying, " Yet to this woman, who faved me and mine from a workhoufe, they wanted me to refufe a home when fhe ftood in need of one ! They need not have been afraid of her being too happy ! Such a mind as hers can never be happy under the confcioufnefs of having been guilty; and could fhe ever forget her crime, one vifit to her poor father would make her remember it again."

Thus did Fanny talk, as I faid before, to thofe who would liften to her ; and there was one auditor who could have liftened to her for ever on this fubject, and who thought Fanny looked more lovely while expreffing her love for her penitent miftrefs, and pleading her caufe with a check flufhed with virtuous indignation, and eyes fuffufed with the tears of artlefs fenfibility, than when, attended by the then happy

Agnes,

Agnes, fhe gave her hand in the bloom of youth and beauty to the man of her heart.

This auditor was a refpectable tradefman who lived in Fanny's neighbourhood, to whom her faithful attachment to Agnes had for fome time endeared her; while Fanny, in return, felt grateful to him for entering with fuch warmth into her feelings, and for liftening fo patiently to her complaints; and it was not long before he offered her his hand.

To fo advantageous an offer, and to a man fo amiable, Fanny could make no objection; efpecially as Agnes advifed her accepting the propofal. But Fanny declared to her lover that fhe would not marry him, unlefs he would promife that Agnes and her child fhould, whenever they chofe, have a home with her. To this condition the lover confented; telling Fanny he loved her the better for making it: and Agnes had foon the fatisfaction of witnefling the union of this worthy couple.

But

But they tried in vain to perfuade **Agnes** to take up her refidence with them. She preferred living by herfelf. To her, folitude was a luxury : as, while the little Edward was playing on the heath with the cottager's children, Agnes delighted to brood in uninterrupted filence over the foothing hope, the fond idea, that alone ftimulated her to exertion, and procured her tranquillity. All the energies of her mind and body were directed to one end ; and while fhe kept her eye ftedfaftly fixed on the future, the paft loft its power to torture, and the prefent had fome portion of enjoyment.

But were not thefe foothing reveries fometimes difturbed by the pangs of ill-requited love ? and could fhe, who had loved fo fondly as to facrifice to the indulgence of her paffion every thing fhe held moft dear, rife fuperior to the power of tender recollection, and at once tear from her heart the image of her fafcinating lover ?

lover ? It would be unnatural to fuppofe that Agnes could entirely forget the once-honoured choice of her heart, and the father of her child ; or that, although experience had convinced her of its unworthinefs, fhe did not fometimes contemplate, with the fick feelings of difappointed tendernefs, the idol which her imagination had decked in graces all its own.

But thefe remembrances were rare. She oftener beheld him as he appeared before the tribunal of her reafon—a cold, felfifh, profligate, hypocritical deceiver, as the unfeeling deftroyer of her hopes and happinefs, and as one who, as fhe had learned from his own lips, when he moft invited confidence, was the moft determined to betray. She faw him alfo as a wretch fo devoid of the common feelings of nature and humanity, that, though fhe left her apartments in London in the dead of night, and in the depth of a fevere winter, an almoft helplefs child in her arms, and no vifible visible protector near, he had never made a single inquiry concerning her fate, or that of his offspring.

At times, the sensations of Agnes bordered on phrensy, when in this heartless, unnatural wretch she beheld the being for whom she had resigned the matchless comforts of her home, and destroyed the happiness and reason of her father.—— At these moments, and these only, she used to rush wildly forth in search of company, that she might escape from herself: but more frequently she directed her steps to the abode of the poor; to those who, in her happier hours, had been supported by her bounty, and who now were eager to meet her in her walks, to repay her past benefactions by a " God bless you, lady !" uttered in a tone of respectful pity.

When her return was first known to the objects of her benevolence, Agnes soon saw herself surrounded by them ; and was, in her humble apparel and dejected state, followed

followed by them with more bleffings and more heartfelt refpect than in the proudeft hour of her profperity.

"Thank God!" ejaculated Agnes, as fhe turned a gliftening eye on her ragged followers; "there are yet thofe whofe eyes mine may meet with confidence. There are fome beings in the world towards whom I have done my duty." But the next minute fhe recollected that the guilty flight which made her violate the duty fhe owed her father, at the fame time removed her from the power of fulfilling her duty to the poor; for it is certain, that our duties are fo clofely linked together, that, as the breaking one pearl from a ftring of pearls hazards the lofs of all, fo the violation of one duty endangers the fafety of every other.

"Alas!" exclaimed Agnes, as this melancholy truth occurred to her, "it is not for me to exult; for, even in the fqualid, meagre countenances of thefe kind and grateful beings, I read evidences of my guilt—

guilt—They looked up to me for aid, and
I deferted them!"

In time, however, thefe acute feelings
wore away ; and Agnes, by entering again
on the offices of benevolence and humanity towards the diftreffed, loft in a confcioufnefs of prefent ufefulnefs the bitter
fenfations of paft neglect.

True, fhe could no longer feed the
hungry or clothe the naked, but fhe could
foften the pangs of ficknefs by expreffing
fympathy in its fufferings. She could make
the naufeous medicine more welcome, if
not more falutary, by adminiftering it herfelf ; for, though poor, fhe was ftill fuperior to the fufferers fhe attended ; and it
was foothing to them to fee fuch a lady
take fo much trouble for thofe fo much
beneath her—and fhe could watch the
live-long night by the bed of the dying,
join in the confoling prayer offered by the
lips of another, or, in her own eloquent
and impaffioned language, fpeak peace
and hope to the departing foul.

H

Thefe

These tender offices, these delicate attentions, so dear to the heart of every one, but so particularly welcome to the poor from their superiors, as they are acknowledgments of the relationship between them, and confessions that they are of the same species as themselves, and heirs of the same hopes, even those who bestow money with generous profusion do not often pay. But Agnes was never content to give relief unaccompanied by attendance: she had reflected deeply on the nature of the human heart, and knew that a participating smile, a sympathizing tear, a friendly pressure of the hand, the shifting of an uneasy pillow, and patient attention to an unconnected tale of twice-told symptoms, were, in the esteem of the indigent sufferer, of as great value as pecuniary assistance.

Agnes, therefore, in her poverty, had the satisfaction of knowing that she was as consoling to the distressed, if not as useful, as she was in her prosperity ; and if there could be a moment when she felt the glow

of

of exultation in her breaſt, it was when ſhe left the habitation of indigence or ſorrow, followed by the well-earned bleſſings of its inhabitants.

Had Agnes been capable of exulting in a conſciouſneſs of being revenged, another ſource of exultation might have been hers, provided ſhe had ever deigned to inquire concerning her profligate ſeducer, whom ſhe wrongfully accuſed of having neglected to make inquiries concerning her and her child. Agnes ſaw, two months after her return from London, an account of Clifford's marriage in the paper, and felt ſome curioſity to know what had ſo long retarded an union which, when ſhe left town, was fixed for the Monday following; and Fanny obſerved an increaſed degree of gloom and abſtraction in her appearance all that day. But, diſmiſſing this feeling from her mind as unworthy of it, from that moment ſhe reſolved, if poſſible, to recall Clifford to her imagination, as one who, towards her, had been guilty not of

H 2   perfidy

perfidy and deceit only, but of brutal and unnatural neglect.

In this laft accufation, however, as I faid before, fhe was unjuft. When Clifford awoke the next morning after his laft interview with Agnes, and the fumes of the wine he had drunk the night before were entirely diffipated, he recollected, with great uneafinefs, the infulting manner in which he had juftified his intended marriage, and the infight into the bafenefs of his character which his unguarded confeffions had given to her penetration.

The idea of having incurred the contempt of Agnes was infupportable. Yet, when he recollected the cold, calm, and dignified manner in which fhe fpoke and acted when he bade her adieu, he was convinced that he had taught her to defpife him ; and, knowing Agnes, he was alfo certain, that fhe muft foon ceafe to love the man whom fhe had once learned to defpife.

"But I will go to her directly," exclaimed

claimed he to himfelf, ringing his bell violently ; "and I will attribute my infernal
folly to drunkennefs." He then ordered
his fervant to call a coach, finding himfelf
too languid, from his late intemperance,
to walk ; and was juft going to ftep into it
when he faw Mrs. Afkew, pale and trembling, and heard her, in a faltering voice,
demand to fee him in private for a few
minutes.

I fhall not attempt to defcribe his rage
and aftonifhment when he heard of the
elopement of Agnes. But thefe feelings
were foon followed by thofe of terror for
her fafety, and that of his child ; and his
agitation for fome moments was fo great
as to deprive him of the power of confidering how he fhould proceed, in order to
hear fome tidings of the fugitives, and endeavour to recall them.

It was evident that Agnes had efcaped
the night before, becaufe a fervant, fitting
up for a gentleman who lodged in the
houfe, was awakened from fleep by the

noife

noife fhe made in opening the door ; and, running into the hall, fhe faw the tail of Agnes's gown as fhe fhut it again ; and looking to fee who was gone out, fhe faw a lady who fhe was almoft certain was mifs Fitzhenry, running down the ftreet with great fpeed. But to put its being Agnes beyond all doubt, fhe ran up to her room, and finding the door open, went in, and could fee neither her nor her child.

To this narration Clifford liftened with fome calmnefs ; but when Mrs. Afkew told him that Agnes had taken none of her clothes with her, he fell into an agony amounting to phrenfy, and exclaiming, " Then it muft be fo—fhe has deftroyed both herfelf and the child !" his fenfes failed him, and he dropped down infenfible on the fofa. This horrible probability had occurred to Mrs. Afkew ; and fhe had fent fervants different ways all night, in order to find her if fhe were ftill in exiftence, that fhe might fpare Clifford, if poffible, the pain of conceiving a fufpicion like her own.

Clifford

Clifford was not fo fortunate as to remain long in a ftate of unconfcioufnefs,
but foon recovered to a fenfe of mifery and
unavailing remorfe. At length, he recollected that a coach fet off that very night
for her native place, from the White-horfe
Cellar, and that it was poffible that fhe
might have obtained a lodging the night
before, where fhe meant to ftay till the
coach was ready to fet off the following
evening. He immediately went to Piccadilly, to fee whether places for a lady and
child had been taken—but no fuch paf-
fengers were on the lift. He then inquired whether a lady and child had gone
from that inn the night before in the coach
that went within a few miles of the town
of ———. But, as Agnes had reached the
inn juft as the coach was fetting off, no
one belonging to it, but the coachman,
knew fhe was a paffenger.

" Well, I flatter myfelf," faid Clifford
to Mrs. Afkew, endeavouring to fmile,
" that fhe will make her appearance here

H 4   at

at night, if she does not come to-day ; and
I will not stir from this spot till the coach
sets off, and will even go in it some way, to
see whether it does not stop to take her
up on the road."

This resolution he punctually put in
practice. All day Clifford was stationed at
a window opposite to the inn, or in the
book-keeper's office ; but night came, the
coach was ready to set off, and still no
Agnes appeared. However, Clifford, having secured a place, got in with the other
passengers, and went six miles or more
before he gave up the hope of hearing the
coachman ordered to stop, in the soft voice
of Agnes.

At last, all expectation failed him; and,
complaining of a violent headach, he desired to be set down, sprang out of the
carriage, and relieved the other passengers
from a very restless and disagreeable companion : and Clifford, without a great coat
and in a violent attack of fever, was wandering on the road to London, in hopes of
meeting

meeting Agnes, at the very time when his victim was on the road to her native place, in company with her unhappy father.

By the time Clifford reached London, he was bordering on a ftate of delirium—but had recollection enough to defire his confidential fervant to inform his father of the ftate he was in, and then take the road to ——, and afk at every inn on the road whether a lady and child (defcribing Agnes and little Edward) had been there. The fervant obeyed ; and the anxious father, who had been informed of the caufe of his fon's malady, foon received the following letter from Wilfon, while he was attending at his bedfide :

    " My lord,

    " Sad news of mifs Fitzhenry and the child ; and reafon to fear they both perifhed with cold. For being told at one of the inns on this road that a young woman and child had been found frozen to

death

death laft night, and carried to the next
town to be owned, I fet off for there directly : and while I was taking a drap of
brandy to give me fpirits to fee the bodies,
for a qualm came over me, when I thought
of what can't be helped, and how pretty,
and good-natured, and happy fhe once
was, a woman came down with a filk
wrapper and a fhawl that l knew belonged
to the poor lady, and faid the young woman found dead had thofe things on.
This was proof pofitive, my lord,——and it
turned me fick. Still it is better fo, than
felf-murder; fo my mafter had beft know
it, I think ; and humbly hoping your lordfhip will think fo too, I remain your lordfhip's

    " Moft humble fervant to command,

               " J. WILSON.

    " P.S. If I gain more particulars, fhall
fend them."

Dreadful as the fuppofed death of Agnes
and her child appeared to the father of
                          Clifford,

Clifford, he could not be sorry that so formidable a rival to his future daughter-in-law was no longer to be feared ; and as Clifford, in the ravings of his fever, was continually talking of Agnes as self-murdered, and the murderer of her child, and of himself as the abandoned cause ; and as that idea seemed to haunt and terrify his imagination, he thought with his son's servant that he had better take the first opportunity of telling Clifford the truth, melancholy as it was. When, therefore, a proper occasion offered he had done so, before he received this second letter from Wilson :

" My lord,

" It was all fudge ;—miss Fitzhenry is alive, and alive like, at ———. She flopped at an inn on the road, and parted with her silk coat and shawl for some things she wanted, and a huffey of a chambermaid stole them and went off in the night with them, and her little by-blow :—but justice overtakes us sooner or later. I suppose his

honour,

honour, my mafter, will be cheery at this;
—but, as joy often diftracts as much as
grief, they fay, though I never believed it,
I take it you will not tell him this good
news hand-over-head,—and am

      " Your lordfhip's
    " Moft humble to command,
            " J. WILSON.

" P. S. I have been to ——, and have
heard for certain mifs F. and her child are
there."

His lordfhip was even more cautious
than Wilfon wifhed him to be; for he refolved not to communicate the glad tidings
to Clifford, cautioufly or incautioufly, as
he thought there would be no chance of
his fon's fulfilling his engagements with
mifs Sandford, if he knew Agnes was living:—efpecially, as her flight and her fuppofed death had proved to Clifford how
neceffary fhe was to his happinefs. Nay,
his lordfhip went ftill further; and he refolved Clifford fhould never know, if he
                      could

could poffibly help it, that the report of her death was falfe.

How to effect this was the difficulty; but wifely conceiving that Wilfon was not inacceffible to a bribe, he offered him fo much a year, on condition he fuffered his mafter to remain convinced of the truth of the ftory that Agnes and her child had perifhed in the fnow, and of intercepting all letters that he fancied came from Agnes; telling him at the fame time that if he ever found he had violated the conditions, the annuity fhould immediately ceafe.

To this Wilfon confented; and, when Clifford recovered, he made his compliance with the terms more eafy, by defiring Wilfon, and the friends to whom his connection with Agnes had been known, never to mention her name in his prefence again, if they valued his health and reafon, and as the fafety of both depended on his forgetting a woman, of whom he had never felt the value fufficiently till he had loft her for ever.

Soon

Soon after, he married ;—and the difagreeable qualities of his wife made him
recollect, with more painful regret, the
charms and virtues of Agnes. The confequence was that he plunged deeper than
ever into diffipation, and had recourfe to
intoxication in order to banifh care and
difagreeable recollections : — and, while
year after year paffed away in fruitlefs expectation of a child to inherit the eftate
and the long-difputed title, he remembered, with agonizing regrets, the beauty
of his loft Edward ; and reflected that, by
refufing to perform his promifes to the injured Agnes, he had deprived himfelf of
the heir he fo much coveted, and of a
wife who would have added dignity to the
title fhe bore, and been the delight and
ornament of his family.

Such were the miferable feelings of
Clifford—fuch the corroding cares that
robbed his mind of its energy, and his body
of health and vigour. Though courted,
careffed, flattered, and furrounded by af-
fluence

fluence and fplendour, he was difappointed
and felf condemned. And, while Agnes,
for the firft time condemning him unjuftly,
attributed his filence and neglect of her
and her offspring to a degree of indifference
and hard-heartednefs which human nature fhudders at, Clifford was feeling all
the horrors of remorfe, without the confo-
lations of repentance.

I have before obferved that one idea
engroffed the mind and prompted the exertions of Agnes ;—and this was the probable reftoration of her father to reafon.—
" Could I but once more hear him call me
by my name, and blefs me with his forgivenefs, I fhould die in peace ; and fomething within me tells me my hopes will not
be vain : and who knows but we may
pafs a contented, if not a happy life together, yet ?—So toil on, toil on, Agnes,
and expect the fruit of thy labours."

Thefe words fhe was in the habit of repeating not only to Fanny and her next
door neighbours (whom fhe had acquainted
with

with her ftory), but to herfelf as fhe fat at work or traverfed the heath. Even in the dead of night fhe would ftart from a troubled fleep, and repeating thefe words, they would operate as a charm on her difturbed mind; and as fhe fpoke the laft fentence, fhe would fall into a quiet flumber, from which fhe awoke the next morning at day-break to purfue with increafed alacrity the labours of the day.

Meanwhile Agnes and her exemplary induftry continued to engage the attention and admiration of the candid and liberal in the town of ———.

Mr. Seymour, who did not venture to inquire concerning her of Fanny while fhe lived at her houfe, now often called there to afk news of Agnes and her employments; and his curiofity was excited to know to what purpofe fhe intended to devote the money earned with fo much labour, and hoarded with fuch parfimonious care.

But Fanny was as ignorant on this fubject

ject as himself, and the only new information she could give him was, that Agnes had begun to employ herself in fancy-works, in order to increase her gains; and that it was her intention soon to send little Edward (then four years old) to town, to offer artificial flowers, painted needle-books, work-bags, &c. at the doors of the opulent and humane.

Nor was it long before this design was put in execution; and Mr. Seymour had the satisfaction of buying the first time all the lovely boy's store, himself, for presents to his daughters. The little merchant returned to his anxious mother, bounding with delight, not at the good success of his first venture, for its importance he did not understand, but at the kindness of Mr. Seymour, who had met him on the road, conducted him to his house, helped his daughters to load his pockets with cakes, &c. and put in his basket, in exchange for his merchandize, tongue, chicken, &c. to carry home to his mother.

Agnes

Agnes heard the child's narration with more pleafure than fhe had for fome time experienced.——"They do not defpife me, then," faid fhe, "they even refpect me too much to offer me pecuniary aid, or prefents of any kind but in a way that cannot wound my feelings."

But this pleafure was almoft immediately checked by the recollection that he whofe wounded fpirit would have been foothed by feeing her once more an object of delicate attention and refpect, and for whofe fake alone fhe could now ever be capable of enjoying them, was ftill unconfcious of her claims to it, and knew not they were fo generally acknowledged. In the words of Jane de Montfort fhe could have faid,

"He to whofe ear my praife moft welcome was,
"Hears it no more!"

"But I will ftill hope on," Agnes ufed to exclaim as thefe thoughts occurred to her; and again her countenance affumed the wild expreffion of a diffatisfied but ftill expecting fpirit.

Three

Three years had now elapfed fince Agnes firft returned to her native place. "The next year," faid Agnes to Fanny with unufual animation, "cannot fail of bringing forth good to me. You know that, according to the rules of the new bedlam, a patient is to remain five years in the houfe : at the end of that time, if not cured, he is to be removed to the apartments appropriated to incurables, and kept there for life, his friends paying a certain annuity for his maintenance; or he is, on their application, to be returned to their care—" —" And what then ?" faid Fanny, wondering at the unufual joy that animated Agnes's countenance. "Why then," replied fhe, " as my father's time for being confined expires at the end of the next year, he will either be cured by that time, or he will be given up to my care; and then, who knows what the confequences may be !"—" What indeed !" returned Fanny, who forefaw great perfonal fatigue and anxiety, if not danger, to Agnes in fuch a plan, a plan, and was going to exprefs her fears and objections; but Agnes, in a manner overpoweringly fevere, defired her to be filent, and angrily withdrew.

Soon after, Agnes received a proof of being ftill dear to her friend Caroline; which gave her a degree of fatisfaction amounting even to joy.

Mr. Seymour, in a letter to his daughter, had given her an account of all the proceedings of Agnes, and expreffed his furprife at the eagernefs with which fhe laboured to gain money, merely, as it feemed, for the fake of hoarding it, as fhe had then only herfelf and child to maintain; and it was certain her father would always be allowed to remain, free of all expenfes, an inhabitant of an afylum which owed its erection chiefly to his benevolent exertions.

But Caroline, to whom the mind of Agnes was well known, and who had often contemplated with furprife and admiration her boldnefs in projecting, her

promptnefs

promptnefs in deciding, and her ability in
executing the projects fhe had formed ; and
above all that fanguine temper which led
her to believe probable what others only
conceived to be poffible, found a reafon
immediately for the paffion of hoarding
which feemed to have taken poffeffion of
her friend—and, following the inftant im-
pulfe of friendfhip and compaffion, fhe
fent Agnes the following letter, in which
was inclofed a bank note to a confiderable
amount :

"I have divined your fecret, my dear Agnes. I know why you are fo anxious to hoard
what you gain with fuch exemplary induftry.
In another year your father will have been
the allotted time under the care of the medical attendants in your part of the world ;
and you are hoarding that you may be able,
when that time comes, to procure for him
elfewhere the beft poffible advice and affiftance. Yes, yes, I know I am right :—
therefore, left your own exertions fhould
not,

not, in the space of a twelvemonth, be crowned with sufficient success, I conjure you, by our long friendship, to appropriate the inclosed to the purpose in question; and should the scheme which I impute to you be merely the creature of my own brain, as it is a good scheme, employ the money in executing it.

" To silence all your scruples, I assure you that my gift is sanctioned by my husband and my father, who join with me in approbation of your conduct, and in the most earnest wishes that you may receive the reward of it in the entire restoration of your afflicted parent. Already have the candid and enlightened paid you their tribute of recovered esteem.

" It is the *slang* of the present day, if I may be allowed this vulgar but forcible expression, to inveigh bitterly against society for excluding from its circle, with unrelenting rigour, the woman who has once transgressed the salutary laws of chastity; and some brilliant and persuasive, but, in my my opinion; miftaken writers, of both fexes, have endeavoured to prove that many an amiable woman has been for ·ever loft to virtue and the world, and become the victim of proftitution, merely becaufe her firft fault was treated with ill-judging and criminal feverity.

" This affertion appears to me to be fraught with mifchief; as it is calculated to deter the victim of feduction from penitence and amendment, by telling her that fhe would employ them in her favour in vain. And it is furely as falfe as it is dangerous. I know many inftances; and it is fair to conclude that the experience of others is fimilar to mine, of women reftored by perfeverance in·a life of expiatory amendment, to that rank in fociety which they had forfeited by one falfe ftep, while their fault has been forgotten in their exemplary conduct, as wives and mothers.

"But it is not to be expected that fociety fhould open its arms to receive its prodigal children till they have undergone a long

4   and

and painful probation, — till they have practised the virtues of self-denial, patience, fortitude, and industry. And she whose penitence is not the mere result of wounded pride and caprice, will be capable of exerting all these virtues, in order to regain some portion of the esteem she has lost. What will difficulties and mortifications be to her? Keeping her eye steadily fixed on the end she has in view, she will bound lightly over them all; nor will she seek the smiles of the world, till, instead of receiving them as a favour, she can demand them as a right.

"Agnes, my dear Agnes, do you not know the original of the above picture? You, by a life of self-denial, patience, fortitude, and industry, have endeavoured to atone for the crime you committed against society; and I hear her voice saying, 'Thy sins are forgiven thee!' and ill befall the hand that would uplift the sacred pall which penitence and amendment have thrown over departed guilt!"

Such

Such was the letter of Caroline :—a letter intended to fpeak peace and hope to
the heart of Agnes ; to reconcile the of-
fender to herfelf ; and light up her dim eye
with the beams of felf-approbation. Thus
did fhe try to confole her guilty and unhappy friend in the hour of her adverfity
and degradation. But Caroline had given
a ftill *greater* proof of the fincerity of her
friendfhip :—fhe had never wounded the
feelings, or endeavoured to mortify the
felf-love of Agnes in the hour of her profperity and acknowledged fuperiority ; fhe
had feen her attractions, and heard her
praifes, without envy ; nor ever with feeming kindnefs but real malignity related to
her, in the accents of pretended wonder
and indignation, the cenfures fhe had incurred, or the ridicule fhe had excited,—
but in every inftance fhe had proved her
friendfhip ; — a memorable exception to
what are farcaftically termed the friend-
fhips of women.

I

" Yes,—

"Yes, — she has indeed divined my secret," said Agnes when she had perused the letter, while tears of tenderness trickled down her cheeks, " and she deserves to assist me in procuring means for my poor father's recovery,— an indulgence which I should be jealous of granting to any one else, except you, Fanny," she added, seeing on Fanny's countenance an expression of jealousy of this richer friend ; " and on the strength of this noble present," looking with a smile at her darned and pieced, though neat apparel, " I will treat myself with a new gown."—" Not before it was wanted," said Fanny peevishly.—" Nay," replied Agnes with a forced smile, " surely I am well dressed enough for a runaway daughter. ' My father loved to see me fine,' as poor Clarissa says, and had I never left him, I should not have been forced to wear such a gown as this :—but, Fanny, let me but see him once more capable of knowing me, and of loving me,

if

if it be poffible for him to forgive me," added fhe in a faltering voice, " and I will then, if he wifhes it, be fine again, though I work all night to make myfelf fo."

" My dear, dear lady," faid Fanny for-rowfully, " I am fure I did not mean any thing by what I faid ; but you have fuch a way with you, and talk fo fadly !—Yet, I can't bear, indeed I can't, to fee fuch a lady in a gown not good enough for me ; and then to fee my young mafter no bet-ter dreffed than the cottager's boys next door ;—and then to hear them call mafter Edward little Fitzhenry, as if he was not their betters ;—I can't bear it—it does not fignify talking, I can't bear to think of it."

" How, then," anfwered Agnes in a fo-lemn tone, and grafping her hand as fhe fpoke, " how can I bear to think of the guilt which has thus reduced fo low both me and my child ? O ! would to God ! my boy could exchange fituation with the children whom you think his inferiors ! I have given him life, indeed, but not one

legal

legal claim to what is neceſſary to the
ſupport of life, except the ſcanty pittance
I might, by a public avowal of my ſhame,
wring from his father."

" I would beg my bread with him
through the ſtreets before you ſhould do
that," haſtily exclaimed Fanny, " and, for
the love of God, ſay no more on this ſub-
ject;—he is *my child,* as well as yours,"
ſhe continued, ſnatching little Edward to
her boſom, who was contentedly playing
with his top at the door; and Agnes, in
contemplating the blooming graces of the
boy, forgot he was an object of compaſſion.

The next year paſſed away as the former had done; and at the end of it Fitzhenry being pronounced incurable, but
perfectly quiet and harmleſs, Agnes de-
ſired, in ſpite of the advice and entreaties
of the governors, that he might be delivered up to her, that ſhe might put him
under the care of Dr. W——.

Luckily for Agnes, the aſſignees of
her father recovered a debt of a hundred
pounds,

pounds, which had long been due to him; and this fum they had great pleafure in paying Agnes, in order to further the fuc-cefs of her laft hope.

On the day fixed for Fitzhenry's releafe, Agnes purchafed a complete fuit of clothes for him, fuch as he ufed to wear in former days, and dreffed herfelf in a manner fuited to her birth, rather than her fituation; then fet out in a poft-chaife, attended by the friendly cottager, as it was judged imprudent for her to travel with her father alone, to take up Fitzhenry at the bedlam, while Fanny was crying with joy to fee her dear lady looking like herfelf again, and travelling like a *gentlewoman.*

But the poor, whom gratitude and affection made conftantly obfervant of the actions of Agnes, were full of confternation, when fome of them heard, and communicated to the others, that a poft-chaife was ftanding at mifs Fitzhenry's door. "O dear! fhe is going to leave us again; what fhall we do without her?" was the

general

general exclamation ; and when Agnes
came out to enter her chaise, she found it
surrounded by her humble friends, lamenting and inquiring, though with cautious
respect, whether she ever meant to come.
back again. "Fanny will tell you every.
thing," said Agnes, overcome with grateful emotion at observing the interest she
excited. Unable to say more, she waved
her hand as a token of farewell to them,
and the chaise drove off.

"Is miss Fitzhenry grown *rich* again ?"
was the general question addressed to
Fanny ; and I am sure it was a disinterested
one, and that, at the moment, they asked
it without a view to their profiting by her
change of situation, and merely as anxious
for her welfare ; and when Fanny told them
whither and wherefore Agnes was gone,
could prayers, good wishes, and bless-
ings, have secured success to the hopes of
Agnes, her father, even as soon as she
stopped at the gate of the bedlam, would
have recognized and received her with

open

open arms. But when she arrived, she found
Fitzhenry as irrational as ever, though delighted to hear he was going to take a ride
with " *the lady*," as he always called Agnes;
and she had the pleasure of seeing him seat
himself beside her with a look of uncommon
satisfaction. Nothing worth relating happened on the road. Fitzhenry was very
tractable, except at night, when the cottager, who slept in the same room with
him, found it difficult to make him keep
in bed, and was sometimes forced to call
Agnes to his assistance; at sight of her
he always became quiet, and obeyed her
implicitly.

The skilful and celebrated man to whom
she applied, received her with sympathizing
kindness, and heard her story with a degree of interest and sensibility peculiarly
grateful to the afflicted heart. Agnes related with praise-worthy ingenuousness the
whole of her sad history, judging it necessary that the doctor should know the

cause

caufe of the malady for which he was to prefcribe.

It was peculiarly the faculty of Agnes to intereft in her welfare thofe with whom fhe converfed ; and the doctor foon expe-rienced a more than ordinary earneftnefs to cure a patient fo interefting from his misfortunes, and recommended by fo in-terefting a daughter. "Six months," faid he, " will be a fufficient time of trial ; and in the mean while you fhall refide in a lodging near us." Fitzhenry then be-came an inmate of the doctor's houfe ; Agnes took poffeffion of apartments in the neighbourhood ; and the cottager returned to ———.

The enfuing fix months were paffed by Agnes in the foul-fickening feeling of hope deferred : and, while the air of the place agreed fo well with her father that he became fat and healthy in his appear-ance, anxiety preyed on her delicate frame, and made the doctor fear that when he

fhould

fhould be forced to pronounce his patient
beyond his power to cure, fhe would fink
under the blow; unlefs the hope of being
ftill ferviceable to her father fhould fupport
her under its preffure. He refolved, therefore, to inform her, in as judicious and
cautious a manner as poffible, that he faw
no profpeɛt of curing the thoroughly fhat-
tered intelleɛt of Fitɀhenry.

" *I* can do nothing for your father," faid
he to Agnes (when he had been under
his care fix months), laying great ftrefs on
the word *I*;———(Agnes, with a face of
horror, ftarted from her feat, and laid
her hand on his arm)———" but *you* can
do a great deal."—

" Can I ? can I ?" exclaimed Agnes,
fobbing convulfively .—" Bleffed hearing !
But the means—the means ?"

" It is very certain," he replied, " that
he experiences great delight when he fees
you, and fees you too employed in his fervice ;—and when he lives with you, and

I 5

fees

fees you again where he has been accuftomed to fee you———"

" You advife his living with me then ?"
interrupted Agnes with eagernefs.——

" I do, moft ftrenuoufly," replied the
doctor.

" Bleffings on you for thofe words !"
anfwered Agnes : " they faid you would
oppofe it ! you are a wife and a kind-
hearted man !"

" My dear child," rejoined the doctor,
" when an evil can't be cured, it fhould at
leaft be alleviated."

" You think it can't be cured, then ?"
again interrupted Agnes.

" Not abfolutely fo :——I know not what
a courfe of medicine, and living with you
as much in your old way as poffible, may do
for him. Let him refume his ufual habits,
his ufual walks, live as near your former
habitation as you poffibly can ; let him
hear his favourite fongs, and be as much
with him as you can contrive to be ; and

if

if you fhould not fucceed in making him rational again, you will at leaft make him happy."

" Happy !—I make him happy, now !" exclaimed Agnes, pacing the room in an agony :—" I made him happy once !—but now !—" '

" You muft hire fome one to fleep in the room with him," refumed the doctor.

" No, no," cried Agnes impatiently ;— " no one fhall wait on him but myfelf ;—I will attend him day and night."

" And fhould your ftrength be worn out by fuch inceffant watching, who would take care of him then ?—Remember, you are but mortal."—Agnes fhook her head, and was filent.—" Befides, the ftrength of a man may fometimes be neceffary, and, for his fake as well as yours, I muft infift on being obeyed."

" You fhall be obeyed," faid Agnes mournfully.

" Then now," rejoined he, " let me give you my advice relative to diet, medicine,

I 6 and

and management." This he did in detail, as he found Agnes had a mind capacious enough to understand his system; and promising to answer her letters immediately, whenever she wrote to him for advice, he took an affectionate farewell of her; and Agnes and her father, accompanied by a man whom the doctor had procured for the purpose, set off for ———.

Fanny was waiting at the cottage with little Edward to receive them,—but the dejected countenance of Agnes precluded all necessity of asking concerning the state of Fitzhenry. Scarcely could the caresses and joy her child expressed at seeing her call a smile to her lips; and, as she pressed him to her bosom, tears of bitter disappointment mingled with those of tenderness.

In a day or two after, Agnes, in compliance with the doctor's desire, hired a small tenement very near the house in which they formerly lived; and in the garden of which, as it was then empty,

9   they

they obtained leave to walk. She also
procured a perſon to ſleep in the room
with her father inſtead of the man who
came with them; and he carried back a
letter from her to the doctor, informing
him that ſhe had arranged every thing according to his directions.

It was a moſt painfully pleaſing ſight to
behold the attention of Agnes to her father.
She knew it was not in her power to re-
pair the enormous injury ſhe had done
him, and that all ſhe could now do, was
but a poor amends; ſtill it was affecting to
ſee how anxiouſly ſhe watched his ſteps
whenever he choſe to wander alone from
home, and what pains ſhe took to make
him neat in his appearance, and cleanly
in his perſon. Her child and herſelf were
clothed in coarſe apparel, but ſhe bought
for her father every thing of the beſt ma-
terials; and, altered as he was, Fitzhenry
ſtill looked like a gentleman.

Sometimes he ſeemed in every reſpect ſo
like

like himfelf, that Agnes, hurried away by
her imagination, would, after gazing on
him fome minutes, ftart from her feat,
feize his hand, and, breathlefs with hope,
addrefs him as if he were a rational being ;
—when a laugh of vacancy, or a fpeech
full of the inconfiftency of phreufy, would
fend her back to her chair again, with a
pulfe quickened, and a check flufhed with
the fever of difappointed expectation.

However, he certainly was pleafed with
her attentions,—but, alas! he knew not
who was the beftower of them : he knew
not that the child whofe ingratitude or
whofe death he ftill lamented in his ravings
in the dead of night, was returned to fuc-
cour, to footh him, and to devote herfelf entirely to his fervice. He heard her,
but he knew her not ; he faw her, but in
her he was not certain he beheld his child :
and this was the pang that preyed on the
check and withered the frame of Agnes :
but fhe perfifted to hope, and patiently
                                    endured

endured the pain of to-day, expecting the joy of to-morrow ; nor did her hopes always appear ill founded.

The first day that Agnes led him to the garden once his own, he ran through every walk with eager delight ; but he seemed surprised and angry to see the long grass growing in the walks, and the few flowers that remained choked up with weeds,— and began to pluck up the weeds with hasty violence.

" It is time to go home," said Agnes to him just as the day began to close in ; and Fitzhenry immediately walked to the door which led into the house, and, finding it locked, looked surprised : then, turning to Agnes, he asked her if she had not the key in her pocket ; and on her telling him that was not his home, he quitted the house evidently with great distress and reluctance, and was continually looking back at it, as if he did not know how to believe her.

On this little circumstance poor Agnes lay ruminating the whole night after, with
joyful

joyful expectation ; and fhe repaired to
the garden at day-break, with a gardener
whom fhe hired, to make the walks look
as much as poffible as they formerly did.
But they had omitted to tie up fome ftraggling flowers ;—and when Agnes, Fanny,
and the cottager, accompanied Fitzhenry
thither the next evening, he, though he
feemed confcious of the improvement that
had taken place, was diflurbed at feeing fome
gilliflowers trailing along the ground ; and
fuddenly turning to Agnes he faid, " Why
do you not bind up thefe ?"

To do thefe little offices in the garden,
and keep the parterre in order, was formerly Agnes's employment. What delight, then, muft thefe words of Fitzhenry, fo evidently the refult of an affo-
ciation in his mind between her and his
daughter, have excited in Agnes ! With
a trembling hand and a glowing cheek fhe
obeyed ; and Fitzhenry faw her, with ma-
nifeft fatisfaction, tie up every ftraggling
flower in the garden, while he eagerly
followed

followed her, and bent attentively over her.

At laft, when fhe had gone the whole round of the flower-beds, he exclaimed, " Good girl ! Good girl !" and, putting his arm round her waift, fuddenly kiffed her cheek.

Surprife, joy, and an emotion difficult to be defined, overcame the irritable frame of Agnes, and fhe fell fenfelefs to the ground. But the care of Fanny foon recovered her again ;—and the firft queftion fhe afked was, how her father (whom fhe faw in great agitation running round the garden) behaved when he faw her fall.

" He raifed you up," replied Fanny, " and feemed fo diftreffed ! he would hold the falts to your nofe himfelf, and would fcarcely fuffer me to do any thing for you ; but, hearing you mutter ' Father ! dear father !' as you began to come to yourfelf, he changed colour, and immediately began to run round the garden, as you now fee him."

" Say

" Say no more, say no more, my dear friend," cried Agnes; " it is enough. I am happy, quite happy;—it is clear that he knew me;—and I have again received a father's embrace:—Then his anxiety too while I was ill;—O! there is no doubt now that he will be quite himself in time."

" Perhaps he may," replied Fanny;— " but——"

" But! and perhaps!" cried Agnes pettishly;—" I tell you he will, he certainly will recover; and those are not my friends who doubt it." So saying, she ran hastily forward to meet Fitzhenry, who was joyfully hastening towards her, leaving Fanny grieved and astonished at her petulance; but few are the tempers proof against continual anxiety, and the souring influence of still renewed and still disappointed hope : and even Agnes, the once gentle Agnes, if contradicted on this one subject, became angry and unjust.

But she was never conscious of having
given

given pain to the feelings of another, without bitter regret and an earnest desire of healing the wound she had made ; and when, leaning on Fitzhenry's arm, she returned towards Fanny, and saw her in tears, she felt a pang severer than she had inflicted, and said every thing that affection and gratitude could dictate, to restore her to tranquillity again. Her agitation alarmed Fitzhenry ; and, exclaiming "Poor thing !" he held the smelling-bottle, almost by force, to her nose, and seemed terrified lest she was going to faint again.

"You see, you see," said Agnes triumphantly to Fanny : and Fanny, made cautious by experience, declared her conviction that her young lady must know more of all matters than she did.

But month after month elapsed, and no circumstances of a similar nature occurred to give new strength to the hopes of Agnes ; however, she had the pleasure to see that Fitzhenry not only seemed attached to her, but to be pleased with little Edward.

She

She had indeed taken pains to teach him to endeavour to amuse her father,—but sometimes she had the mortification of hearing, when fits of loud laughter from the child reached her ear, " Edward was only laughing at grandpapa's odd faces and actions, mamma :" and having at last taught him it was wicked to laugh at such things, because his grandfather was not well when he distorted his face, her heart was nearly as much wrung by the pity he expressed ; for whenever these occasional slight fits of phrensy attacked Fitzhenry, little Edward would exclaim, " Poor grandpapa ! he is not well now ;—I wish we could make him well, mamma !" But, on the whole, she had reason to be tolerably cheerful.

Every evening, when the weather was fine, Agnes, holding her father's arm, was seen taking her usual walk, her little boy gamboling before them ; and never, in their most prosperous hours, were they met with curtsies more low, or bows more respectful, than on these occasions ; and

many

many a one grafped with affectionate eagernefs the meagre hand of Fitzhenry, and the
feverifh hand of Agnes ; for even the moft
rigid hearts were foftened in favour of
Agnes, when they beheld the ravages grief
had made in her form, and gazed on her
countenance, which fpoke in forcible language the fadnefs, yet refignation of her
mind. She might, if fhe had chofen it,
have been received at many houfes where
fhe had formerly been intimate ; but fhe
declined it, as vifiting would have interfered with the neceffary labours of the day,
with her conftant attention to her father,
and with the education of her child. "But
when my father recovers," faid fhe to
Fanny, "as he will be pleafed to find
I am not deemed wholly unworthy of notice, I fhall have great fatisfaction in vifiting with him."

To be brief : —— Another year elapfed,
and Agnes ftill hoped ; and Fitzhenry
continued the fame to every eye but
hers : —— fhe every day fancied his fymptoms

ptoms of returning reason increased, and no one of her friends dared to contradict her. But in order, if poſſible, to accelerate his recovery, ſhe had reſolved to carry him to London, to receive the beſt advice the metropolis afforded, when Fitzhenry was attacked by an acute complaint which confined him to his bed. This event, inſtead of alarming Agnes, redoubled her hopes. She inſiſted that it was the criſis of his diſorder, and expected health and reaſon would return together. Not for one moment, therefore, would ſhe leave his bedſide, and ſhe would allow herſelf neither food nor reſt, while with earneſt attention ſhe gazed on the faſt ſinking eyes of Fitzhenry, eager to catch in them an expreſſion of returning recognition.

One day, after he had been ſleeping ſome time, and ſhe, as uſual, was attentively watching by him, Fitzhenry ſlowly and gradually awoke ; and, at laſt, raiſing himſelf on his elbow, looked round him

with

with an expreffion of furprife, and, feeing Agnes, exclaimed, " My child! are you there? Gracious God! is this poffible?"

Let thofe who have for years been pining away life in fruitlefs expectation, and who fee themfelves at laft poffeffed of the long-defired bleffing, figure to themfelves the rapture of Agnes.—" He knows me! He is himfelf again!" burft from her quivering lips—unconfcious that it was too probable, reftored reafon was here the forerunner of diffolution.

" O! my father!" fhe cried, failing on her kneës, but not daring to look up at him, " O! my father, forgive me, if poffible:—I have been guilty, but I am penitent!"

Fitzhenry, as much affected as Agnes, faltered out, " Thou art reftored to me,—and God knows how heartily I forgive thee!" Then raifing her to his arms, Agnes, happy in the fulfilment of her utmoft wifhes, felt herfelf once more preffed to the bofom of the moft affectionate of fathers.

" But

" But furely you are not now come back?" afked Fitzhenry. " I have feen you before, and very lately."—" Seen me! O yes!" replied Agnes with paffionate rapidity;—" for thefe laft five years I have feen you daily; and for the laft two years you have lived with me, and I have worked to maintain you!"—" Indeed!" anfwered Fitzhenry:—" but how pale and thin you are! you have worked too much:—Had you no *friends*, my child?"

" O yes! and guilty as I have been, they pity, nay, they refpect me, and we may yet be happy! as Heaven reftores you to my prayers!—True, I have fuffered much; but this bleffed moment repays me;—this is the only moment of true enjoyment I have known fince I left my home and you!"

Agnes was thus pouring out the hafty effufions of her joy, unconfcious that Fitzhenry, overcome with affection, emotion, and, perhaps, forrowful recollections, was ftruggling in vain for utterance:—At laft,
—" For

—" For fo many years,—and I knew you not !—worked for me,—attended me !——Blefs, blefs her, Heaven !" he faintly articulated ; and, worn out with illnefs, and choaked with contending emotions, he fell back on his pillow and expired !

Thus, that blefting, the hope of obtaining which alone gave Agnes courage to endure contumely, poverty, fatigue, and forrow, was for one moment her own, and then fnatched from her for ever !

No wonder, then, that when convinced her father was really dead, fhe fell into a flate of flupefaction, from which fhe never recovered ;—and, at the fame time, were borne to the fame grave, the father and daughter.

The day of their funeral was indeed a melancholy one :—They were attended to the grave by a numerous procefion of refpectable inhabitants of both fexes,—while the afflicted and lamenting poor followed mournfully at a diftance. Even thofe who had diftinguifhed themfelves by their vic-

lence

lence againſt Agnes at her return, dropped a
tear as they ſaw her borne to her long
home.   Mrs. Macfiendy forgot her beauty
and accompliſhments in her misfortunes
and early death ; and the mother of the
child who had fled from the touch of
Agnes, felt ſorry that ſhe had ever called
her the wickedeſt woman in the world.

But the moſt affecting part of the proceſſion was little Edward, as chief mourner,
led by Fanny and her huſband, in all the
happy inſenſibility of childhood, uncon-
ſcious all the while that he was the piti-
able hero of that ſhow, which, by its no-
velty and parade, ſo much delighted him,
—while his ſmiles, poor orphan ! excited
the tears of thoſe around him.

Juſt before the proceſſion began to
move, a poſt chariot and four, with white
favours, drove into the yard of the largeſt
inn in the town.   It contained lord and
lady Mountcarrol, who were married only
the day before, and were then on their
way to her ladyſhip's country ſeat.

His

His lordſhip, who ſeemed incapable of reſting in one place for a minute together, did nothing but ſwear at the poſtillions for bringing them that road, and expreſs an earneſt deſire to leave the town again as faſt as poſſible.

While he was gone into the ſtable, for the third time, to ſee whether the horſes were not ſufficiently refreſhed to go on, a waiter came in to aſk lady Mountcarrol's commands, and at that moment the funeral paſſed the window. The waiter (who was the very ſervant that at Mr. Seymour's had refuſed to ſhut the door againſt Agnes, inſtantly turned away his head, and burſt into tears. This excited her ladyſhip's curioſity ; and ſhe drew from him a ſhort but full account of Agnes and her father.

He had ſcarcely finiſhed his ſtory when lord Mountcarrol came in, ſaying the carriage was ready ; and no ſooner had his bride begun to relate to him the ſtory ſhe had juſt heard, than he exclaimed, in

K 2　　　　　　a voice

a voice of thunder, " It is as falfe as hell, madam ! Mifs Fitzhenry and her child both died years ago." Then rufhing into the carriage, he left lady Mountcarrol terrified and amazed at his manner. But when fhe was feating herfelf by his fide, fhe could not help faying that it was impoffible for a ftory to be falfe, which all the people in the inn averred to be true : then, as he did not offer to interrupt her, fhe went through the whole ftory of Agnes and her fufferings ; and fhe was going to comment on them, when the proceffion, returning from church, croffed the road in which they were going, and obliged the poftillions to ftop.

Foremoft came the little Edward, with all his mother's beauty in his face. " Poor little orphan !" faid lady Mountcarrol, giving a tear to the memory of Agnes : " See, my lord, what a lovely boy !" As fhe fpoke, the extreme elegance of the carriage attracted Edward's attention, and fpringing from Fanny's hand, who in vain

endeavoured

endeavoured to hold him back, he ran up
to the door to examine the figures on the
pannel. At that inftant lord Mountcarrol
opened the door, lifted the child into the
chaife, and, throwing his card of addrefs
to the aftonifhed mourners, ordered the
fervants to drive on as faft as poffible.

They did fo in defpite of Mr. Seymour
and others, for aftonifhment had at firft
deprived them of the power of moving;
and the horfes, before the witneffes of this
fudden and ftrange event had recovered
their recollection, had gone too far to
allow themfelves to be ftopped.

The card with lord Mountcarrol's name
explained what at firft had puzzled and
confounded, as well as alarmed them;
and Fanny, who had fainted at fight of
his lordfhip, becaufe fhe knew him, altered as he was, to be Edward's father, and
the bane of Agnes, now recovering herfelf, conjured Mr. Seymour to follow his
lordfhip immediately, and tell him Edward
was bequeathed to her care.

K 3

Mr.

Mr. Seymour inftantly ordered poft-horfes, and in about an hour after fet off in purfuit of the ravifher.

But the furprife and confternation of Fanny and the reft of the mourners, were not greater than that of lady Mountcarrol at fight of her lord's ftrange conduct.——
" What does this outrage mean, my lord ?" fhe exclaimed in a faltering voice ; " and whofe child is that ?"——" It is *my child,* madam," replied he ; " and I will never refign him but with life." Then preffing the aftonifhed child to his bofom, he for fome minutes fobbed aloud,——while lady Mountcarrol, though fhe could not help feeling compaffion for the agony which the feducer of Agnes muft experience at fuch a moment, was not a little difpleafed and fhocked at finding herfelf the wife of that Clifford, whofe name fhe had fo lately heard coupled with that of a villain.

But her attention was foon called from reflections fo unpleafant by the cries of Edward, whofe furprife at being feized and
carried

carried away by a ftranger now yielded to terror, and who, burfting from lord Mount-carrol, defired to go back to his mamma Fanny, and Mr. Seymour.

"What! and leave your own father, Edward?" afked his agitated parent.—— "Look at me,—I am your father;—but, I fuppofe, your mother, as well fhe might, taught you to hate me?"—"My mamma told me it was wicked to hate any body; and I am fure I have no papa: I had a grandpapa, but he is gone to heaven, along with my mamma, Fanny fays, and fhe is my mamma now." And again fcreaming and ftamping with impatience, he infifted on going back to her.

But at length, by promifes of riding on a fine horfe, and of fending for Fanny to ride with him, he was pacified. Then with artlefs readinefs he related his mother's way of life, and the odd ways of his grandpapa; and thus by acquainting lord Mountcarrol with the fufferings and the virtuous exer-tions of Agnes, he increafed his horror of

K 4   his

his own conduct, and his regret at not
having placed so noble-minded a woman
at the head of his family. But whence
arose the story of her death he had yet to
learn.

In a few hours they reached the seat which
he had acquired by his second marriage ;
and there too, in an hour after, arrived
Mr. Seymour and the husband of Fanny.

Lord Mountcarrol expected this visit,
and received them courteously ; while Mr.
Seymour was so surprised at seeing the
once healthy and handsome Clifford
changed to an emaciated valetudinarian,
and carrying in his face the marks of habi-
tual intemperance, that his indignation was
for a moment lost in pity. But recovering
himself, he told his lordship that he came
to demand justice for the outrage which he
had committed, and in the name of the
friend to whom miss Fitzhenry had, in case
of her sudden death, bequeathed her child,
to insist on his being restored to her.

" We will settle that point presently,"
replied

replied lord Mountcarrol; "but firſt I conjure you to tell me all that has happened
to her ſince we parted, whoſe name I have
not for years been able to repeat, and
who, as well as this child, I have alſo for
years believed dead."

" I will, my lord," anſwered Mr. Seymour; "but I warn you, that if you have
any - feeling, it will be tortured by the narration."

" If I have any feeling!" cried his lordſhip; "but go on, ſir; from you, ſir—from
you, as as—*her friend*, I can bear any
thing."

Words could not do juſtice to the agonies of lord Mountcarrol, while Mr. Seymour, beginning with Agnes's midnight
walk to ——, went through a recital of
her conduct and ſufferings, and hopes and
anxieties, and ended with the momentary
recovery and death-ſcene of her father.

But when lord Mountcarrol diſcovered
that Agnes ſuppoſed his not making any
inquiries concerning her or the child pro-

ceeded

ceeded from brutal indifference concerning their fate, and that, confidering him as
a monfter of inhumanity, fhe had regarded
him not only with contempt, but abhor-
rence, and feemed to have difmiffed him
entirely from her remembrance, he beat
his breaft, he rolled on the floor in frantic
anguifh, lamenting, in all the bitternefs of
fruitlefs regret, that Agnes died without
knowing how much he loved her, and
without fufpecting that while fhe was fuppofing him unnaturally forgetful of her and
her child, he was ftruggling with illnefs,
caufed by her defertion, and with a dejection of fpirits which he had never, at
times, been able to overcome ; execrating
at the fame time the memory of his father,
and Wilfon, whom he fufpected of having intentionally deceived him.

To conclude.——Pity for the mifery and
compunction of lord Mountcarrol, and a
fenfe of the advantages both in education
and fortune that would accrue to little
Edward from living with his father, prevailed

9

vailed on Mr. Seymour and the husband of Fanny to consent to his remaining where he was ;—and from that day Edward was universally known as his lordship's son,—who immediately made a will, bequeathing him a considerable fortune.

Lord Mountcarrol was then sinking fast into his grave, the victim of his vices, and worn to the bone by the corroding consciousness that Agnes had died in the persuasion of his having brutally neglected her.—That was the bitterest pang of all! She had thought him so vile, that she could not for a moment regret him !

His first wife he had despised because she was weak and illiterate, and hated because she had brought him no children. His second wife was too amiable to be disliked ; but, though he survived his marriage with her two years, she also failed to produce an heir to the title. And while he contemplated in Edward the mind and person of his mother, he was almost frantic with regret that he was not legally his

K 6   son ;

fon ; and he curfed the hour when with fhort-fighted cunning he facrificed the honour of Agnes to his views of family aggrandizement. But, felfifh to the laft moment of his exiftence, it was a con- fcioufnefs of his own mifery, not of that which he had inflicted, which prompted his expreffions of mifery and regret ; and he grudged and envied Agnes the comfort of having been able to defpife and forget him.

Peace

Peace to the memory of Agnes Fitzhenry!—And may the woman who, like
her, has been the victim of artifice, self-
confidence, and temptation, like her endeavour to regain the efteem of the world
by patient fuffering and virtuous exertion;
and look forward to the attainment of it
with confidence! But may fhe whofe
innocence is yet fecure, and whofe virtues
ftill boaft the ftamp of chaftity, which can
alone make them current in the world,
tremble with horror at the idea of liftening to the voice of the feducer!—For,
though the victim of feduction may in
time recover the approbation of others,
fhe muft always defpair of recovering her
own.—The image of a father, a mother, a
brother, a fifter, or fome other fellow-being,
whofe peace of mind has been injured by
her deviation from virtue, will probably
haunt her path through life; and fhe who
might, perhaps, have contemplated with
fortitude the wreck of her own happinefs,

8   is

is doomed to pine with fruitlefs remorfe at the confcioufnefs of having deftroyed that of another.—For, where is the mortal who can venture to pronounce that his actions are of importance to no one, and that the confequences of his virtues or his vices will be confined to himfelf alone?

END OF THE TALE.

POEMS.

EPISTLE

SUPPOSED TO BE ADDRESSED BY

EUDORA, THE MAID OF CORINTH,

TO

HER LOVER PHILEMON,

Informing him of her having traced his Shadow on the Wall while he was sleeping, the Night before his Departure : Together with the joyful Confequences of this Action.

THE ARGUMENT.

——

Dibutades, a potter of Sicyon, first formed likenesses in clay at Corinth, but was indebted to his daughter for the invention....The girl, being in love with a young man who was soon going from her into some remote country, traced out the lines of his face from his shadow on the wall by candle-light....Her father filling up the lines with clay formed a bust, and hardened it in the fire with the rest of his earthen ware.

PLINY, Lib. xxxv.

EPISTLE

FROM

EUDORA, THE MAID OF CORINTH,

TO

HER LOVER PHILEMON.

———

O Love ! it was thy glory to impart
Its infant being to this magic art ;
By thee infpired, the foft Corinthian maid
Her graceful lover's fleeping form pourtray'd.
HAYLEY.

———

YES, I muft write—applaufe to me is vain,
Tho' by admiring multitudes beftow'd,
While my proud triumphs ftill unknown remain
To thee, dear fource from which the bleffings flow'd.

Then let me breathe the tidings in thine ear ;
Learn, how to blefs me Love and Fame agree !
Why art thou abfent at an hour fo dear ?
I hate e'en glory, if unfhar'd by thee.

O

On the fad eve of that unwelcome day
Ordain'd to tear thee from Eudora's arms,
My finking heart, to various fears a prey,
Felt all a lover's exquifite alarms.

Now with flow ftep, and now with frantic fpeed,
Thro' public fcenes or lonely fhades I rov'd,
When, lo! a favouring, pitying Power decreed
That I afleep fhould find the youth I lov'd.

Yes....I beheld thee (hour with bleffings fraught!)
As on thy hand thy fleep-flufh'd cheek repos'd:
Yet I, at firft, by cold decorum taught,
Fled, and with blufhing hafte the portal clos'd.

But foon Affection fondly check'd my flight:
She whifper'd, " View that winning form once more;
Remember, he who lately charm'd thy fight
Will feek at morning's dawn a diftant fhore."

At that idea, frigid caution fled;
To paffion's fway refigning all my foul,
And hurrying back, with timid, trembling tread,
With breath fufpended, to thy couch I ftole.

Long time I ftood in tender thoughts entranc'd,
Gazing uncheck'd,....a new unwonted blifs....
Now to thy cheek my trembling lips advanc'd,
Nor quite beftow'd, nor quite withheld the kifs.

" And

" And muſt that form delight my eyes no more ?"
I ſoftly murmur'd, as regret impell'd,
When, lo ! with rapture never felt before,
I thy dear ſhadow on the wall beheld.

That moment, Love upon his votary ſmil'd,
My hand his ſceptre, and his throne my breaſt ;
He fired the thought which then my grief beguil'd,
And which to future times will make me bleſt.

With eager haſte I ſeiz'd a ſlender wand
Which near the couch a friendly Power had plac'd,
And with a beating heart, a trembling hand,
Along the wall the faithful ſhadow trac'd.

O happy moment ! how my boſom burn'd
With tranſport, rich reward for all my pain,
When, tho' thy head in various poſtures turn'd,
I ſaw the outline ſtill unchang'd remain !

But 'midſt my rapture as I heard thee ſigh,
And half awak'ning ſpeak Eudora's name,
Beheld thee throw thy languid arms on high,
As recollection o'er thy ſenſes came,

Aſham'd to meet thy fond, inquiring eyes,
Aſham'd my ſtrong emotion to reveal,
Again I fled....reſolv'd my new-found prize
E'en from thy knowledge I'd with care conceal....

But

But when I reach'd my home, to Memory's eye
So dear, so precious feem'd the mimic line,
" Hence, hence, referve !" I cried, " vain fcruples, fly
Philemon's heart fhall fhare the joy of mine !"

Ah me ! that promis'd pleafure Fate denied....
When next we met, thou cam'ft to bid farewell !
And I forgot the invention late my pride,
While on thy neck in fpeechlefs grief I fell.

But when, dear youth ! thy laft farewell I heard,
Nor more my living lover met my view,
Thy lifelefs femblance to my mind recurr'd,
And to the prize with breathlefs fpeed I flew.

Then, as Aurora, while o'er finking night
Her radiant hand affumes a fudden fway,
In one vaft urn collecting all her light,
Pours in full ftream at once the flood of day,

So in a moment, fkill'd the gloom to chafe
Which abfence (lovers' night) around me fpread,
Upon the wall beam'd forth thy well-known face,
And from my mind Affliction's darknefs fled.

What tho' I could not on that wall furvey
The youthful crimfon mantling on thy cheek,
Nor bid the forrow-foothing line pourtray
Thofe looks which paffion, valour, genius fpeak....

Ye

Yet, as I gaze, fee Fancy's friendly art
The charms they wanted to my lines fupply,
See the foft magic of her touch impart
Bloom to thy cheek, and luftre to thine eye:

Thus, tho' the orb that gilds the face of night
Is, fages fay, a gloomy mafs alone,
When Phœbus fills her with his radiant light,
She charms our eyes with fplendour not her own.

But foon new hopes my throbbing bofom fway....
I with quick footfteps to my father prefs....
Exclaiming, " Hafte ! the mimic lines furvey,
Whofe magic power has footh'd my fond diftrefs."

And as he wond'ring gaz'd, I cried, " Thy art
Shall ftronger yet Philemon's graces fhow,
Bid his crifp'd curls upon his forehead part,
And fpeak the grandeur of his fwelling brow."

At my entreaty, then with humid clay
The lines he copied which my hand had made,
And to his furnace bore the prize away,
While I the procefs, fir'd with hope, furvey'd.

But not Deucalion felt more joy to fee
Men fpring to being from the ftones he threw,
Than I experienc'd, when a buft of thee
From the Promethean fire my father drew !

Feebly

Feebly would words that burſt of joy reveal,
The image ſeem'd my lover to reſtore !
And ſure thy heart this tender truth can feel ;
Till thou return, 'twill charm me more and more.

The breath of abſence bids faint flames expire,
But fiercer makes a real paſſion burn :
Long ſeparation feeds a lover's fire,
Yet ſtill, too tardy youth, return ! return !

Now hear my triumphs....Soon the tale tranſpir'd,
Soon was it borne upon the wing of Fame,
Till e'en my inmoſt ſoul of praiſe was tir'd,....
For to our roof aſſembled Corinth came.

Grave ſages....heroes with the laurel'd brow,....
E'en gifted bards who breathe the lofty lay
Feel their glad hearts with new ambition glow,
And bid me haſte their features to portray.

My father's art then forms the mimic head,
While to the lyre my honour'd name is breath'd,
While nymphs and ſwains my path with roſes ſpread,
While round my brow are votive garlands wreath'd.

" And, when thy limbs the funeral pile ſhall preſs,
Think not (they cry) thy glory will expire :
Know, future ages ſhall Eudora bleſs,
And hail the art that ſprang from chaſte deſire.

Yes....

Yes....Corinth's pride ! till Time itfelf be o'er,
Throughout the world be thy dear name convey'd,
And let the lover, hero, fage, adore
The tender fkill of the Corinthian maid."

Such homage Corinth to Eudora pays....
But well thou know'ft I fhun, not covet fame ;
From the fond breaft that genuine paffion fways
For ever diftant be Ambition's flame !

Ah ! not with pride, but tendernefs I glow,
When I this offspring of my love behold ;
And round my heart warm tides of tranfport flow,
To which Ambition's boafted fire is cold.

'Tis mine to know, it glads my father's breaft,
His lov'd Eudora's fpreading fame to fee ;
'Tis mine to feel, thus honour'd, thus carefs'd,
I grow more worthy, matchlefs youth ! of thee.

But, deareft boaft ! I've circumfcrib'd the fway
Of ftern-brow'd Death, the world's relentlefs king,....
Unhonour'd god ! to whom none homage pay,
To whom no voices grateful pæans fing.

Yes....now no more this tyrant of mankind
Shall proudly tear from our encircling arms
The forms we love....and leave no trace behind
Of childhood, youth, or manhood's glowing charms.

L   Sav'd

Sav'd by my power from his rapacious hand,
Their image ftill fhall charm in breathing clay ;
With gentle force fhall Memory's fighs command,
And fpite of fate prolong its pleafing fway.

By this bleft art fucceeding chiefs fhall know
What noble features Corinth's heroes bore,
Then, rous'd to valour by each dauntlefs brow,
Shall be themfelves the heroes they adore.

Befides....(for what Invention's wings can bind ?)....
Some gentle maid, infpir'd by love like mine,
In times to come may bright devices find
On the pale clay to bid warm colours fhine.

Creative art improves by flow degrees ;
When firft a mortal's weight ftern Ocean bore,
No fluttering canvas caught the fwelling breeze,
But on a raft he ventur'd from the fhore.

Sure Love alone could urge fo bold a feat !
And he who firft fuch wondrous danger prov'd,
Was fome fond, faithful youth, refolv'd to meet,
Spite of oppofing feas, the maid he lov'd.

Then, in fucceeding years, Love's godhead fought
The art to perfect which to him we ow'd,
And in a votary's ear he breath'd the thought
That on the bark the ufeful fail beftow'd.

Once

Once on a time two faithful lovers dar'd
The varied dangers of the treacherous main,
And fought an ifland where the prieft prepar'd
To join their hands in Hymen's filken chain :

But, as their bark too flowly feem'd to move
For lovers' wifhes o'er the reftlefs wave,
The impatient youth invok'd the God of Love,
Who foon the aid he afk'd in pity gave.

Infpir'd by him, the eager lover tied
Faft to his veffel's head his fair-one's veil,
And lo ! to land they flew !....Hence others tried
Their mimic art, and form'd the fwelling fail.

Thus Fancy (playful power !) the ftory tells :
And as her airy heights I fondly climb,
Urg'd by the magic of her potent fpells,
I boldly bound acrofs the gulph of Time ;

And as the future blazes on my fight,
I fcorn the prefent, I forget the paft.
Stay, radiant vifions ! ftill my eyes delight !
Scene following fcene, each lovelier than the laft.

Lo there ! the maid by love like mine infpir'd,
Not only colour to my lines imparts,
See her bold hand to greater deeds is fir'd,
See the whole form to mimic being ftarts !

Hail ! fair creations, burſting on my view !
Kings, heroes, ſages, even gods appear,
At Art's bold touch, aſſuming Nature's hue !
Jove graſps his lightning, Pallas lifts her ſpear !

See, to their temples wond'ring votaries throng ;
The breathing forms they view with timid eye ;
Till, bolder grown, they raiſe the exulting ſong,
And " Lo ! a preſent deity !" they cry.

But when ſhall mortals realize the ſcene ?
Not till ſome virgin learn to love like me :
And ſuch, Philemon, is thy mind, thy mien,
Ages may paſs, yet no youth charm like thee.

Meanwhile my humbler art ſhall pleaſe, ſhall bleſs,
Shall make thy charms and my affection known,
Shall calm the mourner's grief o'er thoſe who preſs
Death's awful bier....ſhall ſoftly ſooth my own.

For when my father's aſhes drink my tears,
I to his reverend image ſtill may kneel,
Still think he all my vows of duty hears,
Still deigns to ſhare each heart-felt joy I feel.

And oh ! ſhould Fate thy early death decree !...,
Hence, falſe idea ! traitor to my heart !
When on thy cheek I Death's pale enſign ſee,
In one embrace we'll meet, no more to part.

Yet,

Yet, for thy country fhouldft thou yield thy breath
I'd try to bid my felfifh forrow ceafe....
A Grecian maid fhould blefs her lover's death,
If that he fell for Liberty and Greece.

But oh ! return, Philemon ! round thy head
I'd rather lovers' wreaths than heroes' twine ;
I dare not grieve if thou fhouldft glory wed,
Yet ftill, lov'd youth, I'd rather call thee mine.

What tho' confoling Fancy paints thee near,
And thee I view tho' feas between us roll ;
Tho' thy fond parting accents ftill I hear,
And tho' thy long, laft look thrills thro' my foul :

Yet ftill thy abfence prompts my ceafelefs figh,
Thy fmiles alone can cheer my drooping heart :
For oh ! when Fame my humble roof drew nigh,
Friendfhip I faw by flow degrees depart.

The fair companions of my lowly youth
With coldnefs praife me, or with malice blame,
And on my heart imprefs this mournful truth,
They forfeit friendfhip, who are dear to fame.

But thou canft make me e'en this lofs defpife,
Bleft fhall I be tho' 'reft of every friend,
For ftill Philemon's and my father's eyes
On me the looks of fond affeƈtion bend.

Our fureſt joys Jove's wiſdom has decreed,
From Love's beſt, neareſt, tendereſt ties ſhall come ;
They of true bliſs the ſacred lamp muſt feed,
They, her ſole prieſts....her only altar, home.

Come then, dear youth ! nor fear the wint'ry wind,
But dauntleſs venture on the foaming tide ;
For ſuch ſtrong fetters Danger's power will bind !
And ſuch a pilot will thy veſſel guide !

Know, that laſt night when Sleep in ſilence reign'd,
And I in reſtleſs, feveriſh ſlumbers dream'd,
Beſide my couch a gentle voice complain'd,
While round me more than morning's ſplendour beam'd.

Starting I woke; when, lo ! my dazzled eyes
A figure rich in youth's firſt charms ſurvey'd,
Like thine his features, ſuch his cheek's rich dyes;
Like thee the wondrous viſion ſeem'd array'd.

Then, with arch ſmiles, he cried, " Sleep, wooing fair !
At laſt I've made that rival power remove....
Know'ſt thou not me ? This fond, voluptuous air,
This ſmile, theſe darts, proclaim the God of Love.

And hark ! the wint'ry winds that loudly roar'd,
Huſh'd by my preſence, ſeem to murmur now ;
To theſe chill plains by my warm breath reſtor'd,
See round thy couch the flowers of ſummer blow !

Now

Now hear, bleft maid ! the joyful news I bring :
Long had I known the tumults of thy heart,
Long hover'd o'er thee with delighted wing,
O'erjoy'd to mark a paffion void of art ;

And when thy breaft with boding anguifh fwell'd,
' Now, now (I cried), her homage I'll repay,'
Then flew to earth....and I thy feet impell'd
To feek the couch where thy Philemon lay.

I, on the wall the deep'ning fhadow threw....
The flender wand befide the couch I plac'd....
I, with nice art the faithful outline drew,
And the lov'd youth with added beauty grac'd.

Nor, maid moft favour'd ! ceafes yet my fmile ;
I come to tell thee, fafe from all alarms,
For of its power I will the wind beguile,
I'll bring Philemon to thy conftant arms.

The halcyon, tamer of the tyrant flood,
By her fad note and azure plumage known,
Shall, at my bidding, on the billows brood,
And guard thy heart from forrows like her own.

For this new proof of favour, let thy hand
Exert its fkill my bounty to repay ;
Upon my altar bid my image ftand,
And try Love's glowing features to pourtray."

This

This faid, away he wing'd his graceful flight....
His ruftling pinions fofteft mufic breath'd....
And as he flew, around the brow of Night
His twining figure fpires of radiance wreath'd.

Then from my couch I fprang with grateful hafte,
Eager the lovely vifion to pourtray :
But tho' I thought I Love's own features trac'd,
Thine, and thine only, could my eyes furvey.

Yet wherefore not? Like thee he feem'd to move,
Save that his form with younger graces glow'd,
And my bold fingers on the God of Love
Thy matchlefs femblance have at laft beftow'd :

But, waving richly, o'er his fhoulder fpreads
One of the fleecy, bounding, fhining wings,
On which he hovers o'er true votaries' heads,
And to their aid divine affiftance brings.

Thofe radiant pinions now for thee expand....
Then why, lov'd youth, thy wifh'd return delay ?
Come, fee the wonders of Eudora's hand,
Come, at Love's breathing femblance homage pay.

Yes....when exulting in his kind decree
Thou com'ft triumphant o'er the conquer'd wind,
We'll feek Love's altar....and, on bended knee,
Around his head will votive garlands bind.

O ! thou

O ! thou haſt much to ſee ! no longer poor,
Our alter'd ſtate our alter'd dwelling ſpeaks ;
And when the needy ſtranger opes our door,
We now can give the friendly aid he ſeeks.

Now, ſight moſt pleaſing to his daughter's eyes,
Coarſe robes no more obſcure my father's mien ;
His ample tunic glows with Tyrian dyes,
And all his native dignity is ſeen....

While down his robe his ſilver ringlets flow,
Their white contraſted with its glowing red,....
So look bright clouds upon the mountain's brow,
When with the ſun's laſt crimſon rays o'erſpread :

And both from poverty and pomp remote,
My veſt....But why ſuch trivial tales impart ?
Haſte to behold the change my words denote !
All, all is alter'd here....except....my heart.

Come....and tho' abſence now my bliſs alloys,
More bright 'twill make the hour of meeting glow ;
Paſt pains ſometimes create our preſent joys....
The rainbow's beauties to the ſtorm we owe,

But till we meet, believe the fond diſtreſs
That abſence brings, in all its force I prove,
Save when againſt my throbbing heart I preſs
The faithful ſemblance of the youth I love.

L 5   SONGS

SONGS,

AND OTHER POETICAL PIECES.

SONGS,

&c.

THE MOURNER.

COME, fmiles ! come, gay attire ! and hide
The fecret fang that tears my breaft !
I'll lay my fable garb afide,
And feem to cold inquirers bleft.
Yes,—I will happy triflers join,
As when grief's dart befide me flew,
And love and all its joys were mine,
And forrow but by name I knew :
 For health I faw in Henry's bloom,
 Nor knew it mark'd him for the tomb.

9

Hard was the ftroke,——but O! I hate
The facred pomp of grief to fhow;
Thron'd in my breaft, in fecret ftate,
Shall live the reverend form of woe:
For obfervation would degrade
The homage to her empire paid.

I hate the tear which pity gives,
I'm jealous of her curious eye;
The only balm my wound receives,
Is from my own unheeded figh.
A face of fmiles, a heart of tears!
So in the church-yard (realm of death)
The turf increafing verdure wears,
While all is pale and dead beneath.

TO THE GLOW-WORM.

GEM of this lone and filent vale,
Treafure of evening's penfive hour,
I come thy fairy rays to hail,
I come a votive ftrain to pour.

Nor chilly damps, nor paths untrod,
Shall from thy fhrine my footfteps fright ;
Thy lamp fhall guide me o'er the fod,
And cheer the gathering mifts of night.

Again thy yellow fire impart,
Lo! planets fhed a mimic day ;
Lo! vivid meteors round me dart,
On weftern clouds red lightnings play !

But I difdain thefe garifh fires,
Sporting on evening's fultry wing ;
Thy humbler light my eye admires,
Thy foft, retiring charms I fing.

Thine is an unobtrufive blaze,
Content in lowly fhades to fhine ;
And much I wifh, while thus I gaze,
To make thy modeft merit mine.

For, long by youth's wild wifhes caft
On the falfe world's tempeftuous fea,
I feek retirement's fhore at laft,
And find a monitor in thee.

SONG OF AN INDOSTAN GIRL.

[This Song was occasioned by the following circumstance :—
Mr. Biggs, the composer and editor of many beautiful
Airs, gave me some time ago a plaintive melody, said to
have been composed and sung by an Indostan girl on
being separated from the man she loved.

She had lived several years in India with an English gentleman to whom she was tenderly attached ; but he, when
about to marry, sent his Indian favourite up the country ;
and as she was borne along in her palanquin, she was
heard to sing the above-mentioned melody. To this
melody I wrote the following words ; and they have been
already given to the public, with the original music, in a
second set of Hindoo airs, arranged and harmonized by
Mr. Biggs.

'TIS thy will, and I must leave thee,
   O ! then, best belov'd, farewell !
I forbear, left I should grieve thee,
   Half my heartfelt pangs to tell.
Soon a British fair will charm thee,
   Thou her smiles wilt fondly woo ;
But tho' she to rapture warm thee,
   Don't forget THY POOR HINDOO.

Well

Well I know this happy beauty
   Soon thy envied bride will fhine ;
But will fhe, by anxious duty,
   Prove a paffion warm as mine ?
If to rule be her ambition,
   And her own defires purfue ;
Thou'lt recall my fond fubmiffion,
   And regret THY POOR HINDOO.

Born herfelf to rank and fplendour,
   Will fhe deign to wait on thee ;
And thofe foft attentions render,
   Thou fo oft haft prais'd in me ?
Yet, why doubt her care to pleafe thee ?
   Thou muft every heart fubdue ;
I am fure, each maid that fees thee
   Loves thee like THY POOR HINDOO.

No, ah ! no !—tho' from thee parted,
   Other maids will peace obtain ;
But thy Zayda, broken-hearted,
   Ne'er, O ! ne'er, will fmile again.
O ! how faft from thee they tear me !
   Fafter ftill fhall death purfue :
But 'tis well—death will endear me,
   And thou'lt mourn THY POOR HINDOO.

SONG.

SONG*.

———

YES, Mary Anne, I freely grant,
The charms of Henry's eyes I fee ;
But while I gaze, I fomething want,
I want thofe eyes—to gaze on me.

And I allow, in Henry's heart
 Not Envy's felf a fault can fee :
Yet ftill I muft one wifh impart,
 I wifh that heart—to figh for me.

————

SONG.

———

A YOUTH for Jane with ardour figh'd,
 The maid with fparkling eye ;
But to his vows fhe ftill replied,
 " I'll hear you by and by."

———

* This and the three following Songs belong to a fet of
Songs compofed by Mr. Biggs, which are now publifhed.

" Sufpenfe

" Sufpenfe (he cries) my bloom decays,
    " And bids my fpirits fly ;
" *Now* hear my vows,"——but ftill fhe fays,
    " I'll hear you by and by."

At length her frowns his love fubdue,
    He fhuns her fcornful eye,
And Emma feeks, who'll hear him woo
    Both now, and by and by.

And foon to church he leads the maid,
    When lo ! he fees draw nigh,
The now repentant fair, who faid
    She'd hear him by and by.

" Hear me (fhe cries) : no more in vain
    " Thy heart for me fhall figh !"——
" I'm bufy now (faid he)——but, Jane !
    " I'll hear you by and by."

A MAD-SONG.

HA ! what is this that on my brow
Preffes with fuch o'erwhelming power ?
My love to heav'n is gone, I know ;
But 'tis to fix our bridal hour.
Then on his tomb why fhould I forrow ?
He's gone, but he'll return to-morrow.

Ah ! then yon lofty hill I'll mount,
And feize on morning's brighteft cloud ;
On that I'll wait my love, and count
The moments till he leaves his fhrowd :
And be the rainbow's veft fhall borrow,
To grace our bridal day to-morrow.

But all's not right in this poor heart,——
Yet why fhould I his lofs deplore ?
It was indeed a pang to part,
But when he comes, he'll rove no more :
And all to day can laugh at forrow,
When fure of being blefs'd to-morrow.

Then why am I in black array'd ?
And why is Henry's father pale ?
And why do I, poor frantic maid,
Tell to the winds a mournful tale ?
Alas ! the weight I feel is forrow....
No, no—he cannot come to-morrow.

————————

SONG.

SONG.

———

I ONCE rejoic'd, sweet Evening gale,
To see thy breath the poplar wave ;
But now it makes my cheek turn pale,
It waves the grafs o'er Henry's grave.

Ah ! setting sun ! how chang'd I seem !
I to thy rays prefer deep gloom,——
Since now, alas ! I see them beam
Upon my Henry's lonely tomb.

Sweet Evening gale ! howe'er I seem,
I with thee o'er my sod to wave ;
Ah ! setting sun ! soon mayst thou beam
On mine, as well as Henry's grave !

———

EPIGRAM

On reading the *Pleadings* of Count LALLY TOLENDAL
for his Father the late Count LALLY.

———

OUI, je conviens qu' Enée étoit digne d'envie,
Mais je crois que Lally le surpasse en bonheur :
Le Troyen à son Père a su sauver LA VIE,
Mais au sien le François a su sauver L'HONNEUR.

LINES

LINES

ADDRESSED TO MR. BIGGS,

On his having fet the MAD SONG, and " MY LOVE
TO WAR IS GOING."

———

WHILE from your tafte my humble lays acquire
Attractive charms to them till now unknown,
My mufe deceiv'd exulting ftrikes her lyre,
And loves her ftrains for graces not their own.

————————

FATHERLESS FANNY.

A BALLAD.

———

KEEN and cold is the blaft loudly whiftling around ;
As cold are the lips that once fmil'd upon me,
And unyielding, alas ! as this hard-frozen ground,
The arms once fo ready my fhelter to be.
Both my parents are dead, and few friends I can boaft,
But few to confole, and to love me, if any ;
And my gains are fo fmall,—a bare pittance at moft
Repays the exertions of fatherlefs Fanny.

Once

Once indeed I with pleafure and patience could toil,
But 'twas when my parents fat by, and approv'd ;
Then my laces to fell I went out with a fmile,
Becaufe my fatigue fed the parents I lov'd.
And at night when I brought them my hardly-earn'd
    gains,
Tho' fmall they might be, ftill my comforts were many ;
For my mother's fond bleffing rewarded my pains,
My father ftood watching to welcome his Fanny.

But, ah ! now that I work by their prefence uncheer'd,
I feel 'tis a hardfhip indeed to be poor,
While I fhrink from the labour no longer endear'd,
And figh as I knock at the wealthy man's door.
Then, alas ! when at night I return to my home,
No longer I boaft that my comforts are many ;
To a filent, deferted, dark dwelling I come,
Where no one exclaims " Thou art welcome, my Fanny."

That, that is the pang ;—want and toil would impart
No pang to my breaft, if kind friends I could fee ;
For the wealth I require is that of the heart,
The fmiles of affection are riches to me.

Then, ye wealthy, O think when to you I apply
To purchafe my goods, tho' you do not buy any,
If in accents of kindnefs you deign to deny,
You'll comfort the heart of poor fatherlefs Fanny.

SONG

SONG—TO LAURA.

MAID of the cold fufpicious heart,
Ah! wherefore doubt thy Henry's love?
Imputing thus to practis'd art
The figns that real paffion prove.

While thro' the fleeplefs night I figh,
And jealous fears and anguifh own,
At morn in reftlefs flumbers lie,
Then, languid, rife to mufe alone :

While harmony my foul difdains,
And beauties vainly round me fhine,
Save when I hear thy fav'rite ftrains,
Or beauties fee refembling thine :

While I in fix'd attention gaze,
If e'er thou breathe thy plaintive lay,
And while, tho' others loudly praife,
I deeply figh, and nothing fay :

While I reject thy offer'd hand,
And fhun the touch which others feek,
Alone with thee in filence ftand,
Nor dare, tho' chance befriend me, fpeak

Ah! Laura, while I thus impart
The ardent love in which I pine,
While all thefe fymptoms fpeak *my* heart,
Say, why fhould doubt inhabit *thine* ?

THE DESPAIRING WANDERER.

O! 'TIS an hour to mifery dear!
No noife, but dafhing waves, I hear,
Save hollow blafts that rufh around,
For Midnight reigns with horrors crown'd.

Lo! clouds in fwarthy grandeur fweep
Portentous o'er the troubled deep :
O'er the tall rocks' majeftic heads,
Lo! billowy vapour flowly fpreads,
While Fancy, as fhe marks its fwell,
Around it throws her magic fpell :——
And fee! fantaftic fhapes feem near,
The rocks with added height appear,
And from the mift, to feek the tide,
Gigantic figures darkly glide ;
While, with quick ftep and hurried mien,
Pale Terror leads the fhadowy fcene.
Again loud blafts I fhudd'ring hear,
Which feem to Fancy's lift'ning ear
To toll fome fhipwreck'd failor's knell!
Of fear, of grief, of death, they tell.
Perhaps they bade yon foaming tide
Unheard-of mifery fcatter wide.
Hail! dread idea, fancy taught,——
To me with gloomy pleafure fraught ;

M.   I fhould

I fhould rejoice the world to fee
Diftrefs'd, diftracted, loft, like me.

O ! why is phrenfy call'd a curfe ?
I deem the fenfe of mifery worfe :
Come, Madnefs, come ! tho' pale with fear
Be joy's flufh'd cheek when thou art near,.
On thee I eager glances bend ;
Defpair, O Madnefs ! calls thee friend !
Come, with thy vifions cheer my gloom,—
Spread o'er my cheek thy feverifh bloom !
To my weak form thy ftrength impart,
From my funk eye thy lightnings dart !
Oh ! come, and on the troubled air
Throw rudely my diforder'd hair ;
Arm me with thy fupporting pride,
Let me all ills, all fears deride !
Oh ! bid me roam in tatter'd veft,
Bare to the wint'ry wind my breaft,
Horrors with dauntlefs eye behold,
And ftalk in fancied greatnefs bold !
Let me, from yonder frowning rock,
With thy fhrill fcream the billows mock ;
With fearlefs ftep afcend the fteep,
That totters o'er th' encroaching deep ;
And while the fwelling main along
Blue lightning's awful fplendours throng ;
And while upon the foaming tide
Danger and Death in triumph ride,

And

And thunder rends the ear of Night,
Rouſing the form of pale Affright,
Let me the mountain torrent quaff,
And 'midſt the war of nature—laugh!

THE ORPHAN BOY'S TALE.

STAY! lady, ſtay, for mercy's ſake,
And hear a helpleſs orphan's tale!
Ah! ſure my looks muſt pity wake,—
'Tis want that makes my cheek ſo pale.
Yet I was once a mother's pride,
And my brave father's hope and joy;
But in the Nile's proud fight he died,
And I am now an ORPHAN BOY.

Poor fooliſh child! how pleas'd was I,
When news of Nelſon's victory came,
Along the crowded ſtreets to fly
And ſee the lighted windows flame!—
To force me home my mother ſought,
She could not bear to ſee my joy;
For, with my father's life 'twas bought,
And made me a poor ORPHAN BOY.

9

The people's ſhouts were long and loud,——
My mother, ſhudd'ring, cloſ'd her ears,——
" Rejoice ! rejoice !" ſtill cried the crowd :
My mother anſwer'd with her tears.
" Why are you crying thus," ſaid I,
" While others laugh and ſhout with joy ?"
She kiſs'd me——and with ſuch a ſigh !
She call'd me her poor ORPHAN BOY !

" What is an orphan boy ?" I ſaid,——
When ſuddenly ſhe gaſp'd for breath,
And her eyes cloſ'd ;——I ſhriek'd for aid,
But, ah ! her eyes were cloſ'd in death.
My hardſhips ſince I will not tell :
But, now no more a parent's joy,
Ah ! lady,——I have learnt too well,
What 'tis to be an ORPHAN BOY.

O ! were I by your bounty fed !
Nay, gentle lady, do not chide,——
Truſt me, I mean to earn my bread ;
The ſailor's orphan boy has pride.——
Lady, you weep !——Ha !——this to me ?
You'll give me clothing, food, employ ?——
Look down, dear parents ! look, and ſee
Your happy, happy, ORPHAN BOY.

THE END.

Printed by Davis, Wilks, and Taylor, Chancery-lane.

WS - #0018 - 111122 - C0 - 229/152/15 - PB - 9780371161746 - Gloss Lamination